NURSING LEADERSHIP AND MANAGEMENT

SECOND EDITION

Maureen P. Sullivan, RN, MSN
Assistant Professor of Nursing
Villanova University
Villanova, Pennsylvania

Springhouse Corporation
Springhouse, Pennsylvania

Staff

Executive Director, Editorial
Stanley Loeb

Senior Publisher, Trade and Textbooks
Minnie B. Rose, RN, BSN, MEd

Art Director
John Hubbard

Clinical Consultants
Maryann Foley, RN, BSN; Patricia Kardish Fischer, RN, BSN

Editors
David Moreau, Diane Labus, Carol Munson

Copy Editors
Diane M. Armento, Debra Davis, Pamela Wingrod

Designers
Stephanie Peters (associate art director),
Jacalyn Facciolo (book designer), Maryanne
Buschini

Typography
Diane Paluba (manager), Elizabeth Bergman, Joyce
Rossi Biletz, Phyllis Marron, Robin Mayer, Valerie L.
Rosenberger

Manufacturing
Deborah Meiris (director), Anna Brindisi, T.A. Landis

Editorial Assistants
Caroline Lemoine, Louise Quinn, Betsy K. Snyder

℞ A member of the Reed Elsevier plc group

Printed in the United States of America. For information,
write Springhouse Corporation, 1111 Bethlehem Pike,
P.O. Box 908, Springhouse, PA 19477-0908.

SNLM-011094

Library of Congress Cataloging-in-Publication Data

Sullivan, Maureen P.
  Nursing leadership and management /
Maureen P. Sullivan — 2nd ed.
    p. cm. — (Springhouse notes)
  Includes bibliographical references and
index.
    1. Nursing services — Administration —
Outlines, syllabi, etc. 2. Leadership —
Outlines, syllabi, etc. I. Title. II. Series.
    [DNLM: 1. Nursing, Supervisory — outlines.
2. Leadership — nurses' instruction. 3.
Leadership — outlines.   WY 18 S951n 1995]
RT89.S853   1995
610.73′068 — dc20
DNLM/DLC   94-22891
ISBN 0-87434-741-6   CIP

Contents

Advisory Board and Reviewers

REVIEWERS

1st Edition

Judy Carlson-Catalano, RN, EdD
Associate Professor of Nursing
College of Staten Island
Staten Island, N.Y.

2nd Edition

Sheila Myer, RN, MSN
Associate Professor
State University of New York
College at Brockport
Department of Nursing
Brockport, N.Y.

How to Use Springhouse Notes

Springhouse Notes is a multi-volume study guide series developed especially for nursing students. Each volume provides essential course material in an outline format, enabling the student to review the information efficiently.

Special features recur throughout the book to make the information accessible and easy to remember. *Learning objectives* begin each chapter, encouraging the student to evaluate knowledge before and after study. Next, within the outlined text, *key points* are highlighted in shaded blocks to facilitate a quick review of critical information. Key points may include cardinal signs and symptoms, current theories, important steps in a nursing procedure, critical assessment findings, crucial nursing interventions, or successful therapies and treatments. *Points to remember* summarize each chapter's major themes. *Study questions* then offer another opportunity to review material and assess knowledge gained before moving on to new information. Difficult, frequently used, or sometimes misunderstood terms (indicated by small capital letters in the outline) are gathered at the end of each chapter and defined in the *glossary*, Appendix A; answers to the study questions appear in Appendix B.

The Springhouse Notes volumes are designed as learning tools, not as primary information sources. When read conscientiously as a supplement to class attendance and textbook reading, Springhouse Notes can enhance understanding and help improve test scores and final grades.

CHAPTER 1

Overview of Nursing Leadership and Management

Learning objectives

Check off the following items once you've mastered them:

☐ Compare and contrast leadership and management.

☐ Identify the role of leadership within an organization.

☐ Identify the role of management within an organization.

☐ Discuss the historical development of organizational, leadership, and management thought.

☐ List the attributes necessary for effective leadership.

☐ Describe the functions of a nurse leader and a nurse manager.

I. Introduction

A. *Leadership* and *management* are not synonymous terms
  1. A leader uses specific skills to inspire the work of others
  2. A manager coordinates the work of others
  3. All leaders are not necessarily managers
  4. Equally true, all managers are not necessarily leaders

B. An effective manager, however, is one who can identify and learn the skills of leadership

C. In some form, leadership and management are essential to all organizations

D. Understanding the nature of leadership and management within an organization requires an understanding of the organization's structure

E. An organization's structure is determined by its operative organizational theory, which serves as a basis for
  1. Division and specialization of work groups
  2. Number of hierarchical levels
  3. Focus of decision-making authority
  4. Lines of communication

F. The role of leadership within an organization is to ensure that organizational goals are attained while facilitating healthy relationships among group members through communication, group dynamics, decision making, and change

G. The role of management within an organization is to ensure that organizational goals are attained through planning, organizing, directing, and controlling

H. The roles of leader and manager are separate but can blend and overlap; they may include
  1. Client advocate
  2. Decision maker
  3. Educator
  4. Role model
  5. Change agent
  6. Counselor

I. Dramatic changes in health care institutions have created a need to unite leadership and management skills
  1. The nurse leader-manager must possess vision and be able to think in terms of change, renewal, and political and economic realities
  2. The primary function of the nurse leader-manager is to create an environment of trust through competence

II. Historical perspectives

A. General information
  1. Leadership and management issues have been debated for centuries
  2. Elements of leadership and management can be traced through early political and governmental systems
  3. The modern theories of leadership and management arose mainly from research conducted in the late 1800s and early 1900s

B. Early history to the 20th century
  1. Important theorists from ancient to modern times have considered the concepts of organization, leadership, and management
  2. Aristotle, in the 3rd century B.C., saw leadership as an essential component of an organized society
  3. Machiavelli, in the 1500s, identified power as the basis of leadership and management
  4. Adam Smith, in the 1700s, determined that effective management depends on specialization of work tasks

C. Early 1900s
  1. *Classical* organizational theory was developed during this period
  2. This theory holds that the role of management is to increase production by closely supervising the work of others
  3. Leadership theorists of this period were mainly concerned with identifying an effective leader's traits

D. 1920s to 1960s
  1. Ownership's and management's perceived lack of concern for worker satisfaction led organizational theorists to develop *humanistic* organizational theory
  2. In this theory, the role of management encompasses an equal concern for both production and worker satisfaction
  3. Based on the work of such theorists as Peter Drucker, Abraham Maslow, Douglas McGregor, Frederick Hertzberg, and Robert House, motivating employees became a major managerial function
  4. Leadership theorists of this period addressed the issues of task (work PRODUCTIVITY) and relationship (social organization of workers) behaviors and tried to predict how much emphasis should be placed on each of these issues in a given situation to achieve organizational goals

E. 1960s to present
  1. By the 1960s, some theorists became concerned that humanistic organizational theory was incomplete and failed to address such issues as status and roles within organizations
  2. This concern led to the development of *modern* organizational theory
  3. Modern organizational theory holds that management's primary role is to monitor communication within an organization

    4. Under this theory, leadership is viewed as a process of moving groups toward goal achievement and involves interaction among and synthesis of many variables

    5. Leadership theories proposed under this theory have become the foundation for many current principles of leadership and management

III. Leadership

A. General information

    1. Leadership is an interpersonal process involving influence and role modeling that inspires people to achieve personal and group goals

    2. Leadership is a learned behavior

    3. Effective leadership requires a thorough understanding of situational and group dynamics

    4. Leadership is a dynamic process that adapts to different circumstances

    5. An effective leader can assess a situation and determine the most appropriate action to attain group and organizational goals

    6. The leadership role is attained through POWER, authority, and influence

B. Attributes of an effective leader

    1. Self-confidence and self-awareness

    2. Strong personal values and the skill of values clarification, which involves choosing freely from alternatives, prizing the choice made, and acting consistently on that choice

    3. Advocacy, which involves providing information and support to those being led

    4. ACCOUNTABILITY, which involves a willingness to take responsibility for personal values and actions that affect the organization

C. Leadership styles

    1. Leadership style refers to the behavior a leader uses in a specific situation; different situations may require different leadership styles (see *Leadership Styles*)

    2. In AUTOCRATIC LEADERSHIP, the leader exerts virtually total control over group members by issuing orders, demanding obedience, and focusing on productivity

    3. *Bureaucratic leadership* is similar to autocratic leadership but places more emphasis on adhering to rigid rules and procedures

    4. In *parental leadership*, the leader fosters obedience and dependency in group members

    5. In DEMOCRATIC LEADERSHIP, the leader shares control with group members and encourages them to participate in decision making and to cooperate in carrying out decisions

    6. In LAISSEZ-FAIRE LEADERSHIP, the leader relinquishes control, giving group members total freedom in a highly permissive atmosphere

    7. In *multicratic leadership*, the leader moves freely among autocratic, democratic, and laissez-faire styles, depending on the situation

LEADERSHIP STYLES

This chart lists the three most common leadership styles and representative actions and reactions.

LEADERSHIP STYLE	LEADER'S ACTIONS	SUBORDINATE'S REACTIONS
Autocratic (also called authoritative)	Exerts a strong, dogmatic direction and maintains close control over subordinate	• May feel hostile toward the supervisor and criticize decisions because staff were not included in making them
Democratic (also called collaborative, supportive, or participative)	Retains authority and control but supports subordinate's participation in setting policies and goals	• Derives satisfaction from having some decision-making control • Thinks the leader's decisions and tactics are fair because staff participated in making the decisions
Laissez-faire (also called free-rein)	Allows subordinate the chance to set goals without direction, giving subordinate maximum decision-making freedom; serves mainly as a resource	• May feel confused because of the lack of direction

D. Functions of a nurse leader
1. Acts as a role model for others
2. Provides expert nursing care based on theory and research findings
3. Demonstrates knowledge about organizational theory to support and influence organizational policies
4. Collaborates with others to provide optimum health care
5. Assumes responsibility for providing information and support to clients
6. Uses advocacy to help effect changes that will benefit clients and the health care institution
7. Uses the American Nurses Association code of ethics and standards of practice as guidelines for individual and professional accountability

E. Applications to nursing
1. Health care institutions are business organizations concerned with productivity and, in many cases, profitability
2. Today, productivity in health care organizations occurs in an atmosphere of cost containment
3. Nurse leaders should focus on maintaining a high quality of client care and on documenting and publicizing the cost-effectiveness of professional nursing in a health care organization

IV. Management

A. General information
   1. Management involves coordinating and supervising personnel and resources to accomplish organizational goals
   2. Management functions include planning, organizing, directing, and evaluating
   3. Planning, the most critical management activity involves carefully evaluating the situation, setting goals, establishing priorities, and identifying necessary resources

B. Attributes of an effective manager
   1. Sound communication, decision-making, and problem-solving skills
   2. Thorough understanding of such processes as motivation, performance appraisal, quality assurance, and different management methods
   3. Ability to balance sometimes conflicting goals, such as maintaining excellence in work within time and budgetary constraints
   4. Vision to predict and plan for the future
   5. Trust in personnel and use of group dynamic skills to achieve organizational goals
   6. Concern with the task and relationship needs of personnel

C. Functions of a nurse manager
   1. Carefully assesses a situation to determine the optimum course of action
   2. Sets goals for clients or personnel, then establishes priorities and identifies resources needed to achieve these goals
   3. Structures the work load and organizes personnel to use the minimum time and resources necessary to achieve goals
   4. Guides and stimulates clients or personnel to encourage adherence to the plan and progress toward goal achievement
   5. Measures and documents the activity of clients or personnel as they progress toward goal achievement
   6. Uses rewards and disciplinary action as components of the evaluation process

D. Applications to nursing
   1. Health care organizations are demanding managerial expertise at the staff nurse level
   2. Quality client care hinges on effective management of allied health personnel
   3. Innovation and change, two constant factors in any health care organization, must be dealt with at the staff nurse level using good communication and problem-solving skills to plan, direct, organize, and evaluate
   4. In the ever-changing health care field, the staff nurse not only must be clinically competent but also must have managerial skills

Points to remember

Leadership and *management* are not synonymous.

An effective leader possesses the qualities of self-confidence, self-awareness, values clarification, advocacy, and accountability.

Different leadership styles suit different situations.

Management involves planning, organizing, directing, and evaluating.

The staff nurse must have clinical and managerial competency.

Glossary

The following terms are defined in Appendix A, page 110.

accountability

autocratic leadership

democratic leadership

laissez-faire leadership

power

productivity

Study questions

To evaluate your understanding of this chapter, answer the following questions in the space provided; then compare your responses with the correct answers in Appendix B, page 115.

1. What determines an organization's structure? _____

   _____

   _____

2. How does classical organizational theory view the role of management?

   _____

   _____

3. What type of leader fosters obedience and dependency in group members?

   _____

   _____

4. What is the most critical management function? _____

   _____

   _____

CHAPTER 2

Organizational Theories

Learning objectives

Check off the following items once you've mastered them:

☐ Describe the three major organizational theories.

☐ Identify the theory under which most health care organizations operate.

☐ Define *bureaucratic* organizational structure.

☐ Describe the focus of a health care organization operating under a humanistic organizational theory.

I. Introduction

A. The study of organizational structure is accomplished by applying organizational theories
1. The basic principles of current organizational theories have their roots in ancient times
2. Intensive research into organizational structure began during the late 19th century and continues today

B. Organizational theories fall into three basic categories, each of which is characterized by a prevailing school of thought
1. Elements of each school of thought apply to health care organizations today
2. Health care organizations are major industries and as such are structured on various principles of organizational theory

C. Organizational theories have several implications for nursing
1. Understanding organizational structures from historical and scientific perspectives provides a basis for effective nursing leadership and management
2. Nurses must be aware of the evolution of organizational theory to be able to contribute to the organization
3. Knowledge of the theory or theories under which a health care organization functions enables nurses within that organization to clarify their individual roles and functions

II. Classical organizational theory

A. General information
1. The classical school of organizational theory represents the earliest attempt to study organizations scientifically
2. Many theorists have contributed to classical organizational theory
   a. Max Weber, in the late 1800s and early 1900s, developed the concept of a BUREAUCRACY as the ideal form of organization
   b. Frederick Taylor, in 1911, proposed the principles of "scientific management," which focus primarily on improving individual productivity
   c. Henri Fayol, in the 1940s, laid the foundation for the classical management functions of planning, organizing, controlling, and evaluating

B. Key concepts
1. Classical organizational theory is based on the "ideal" formal organizational structure, known as a *bureaucracy,* and on individual productivity

    a. Key elements of a bureaucracy include a centralized authority structure, highly specialized division of labor, rigid hierarchy of management, rigid rules and regulations, routine, formal communications, and detailed record keeping

    b. There is no widely accepted alternative to bureaucracy in health care organizations

  2. Classical organizational theory emphasizes task orientation, efficient operation, and high individual productivity

    a. It views monetary reward as the primary incentive for encouraging high individual productivity

    b. It promotes many levels of management within an organization, with each level overseeing one specific aspect of the work and each employee developing expertise only in a particular task or set of tasks

    c. It also promotes managers' rigid, yet fair, control of employees and employees' strict obedience to those in authority

C. Applications to nursing

  1. Most health care organizations are structured based on applied principles of classical organizational theory

  2. Health care organizations have very specific chains of command, clearly delineated levels of authority, written policies and procedures, and specific rules and regulations for employees

  3. Health care organizations emphasize tasks, efficiency, and productivity in providing client care

    a. The functional and team systems of client care delivery are based on classical organizational theory

    b. Nurses and other personnel receive training, in the form of in-service and orientation, to develop job expertise

    c. Personnel receive monetary rewards for their work

    d. In the future, health care organizations may become more flexible structures with decentralized authority

III. Humanistic organizational theory

A. General information

  1. Questions about the rigid management structure and lack of concern for employee welfare emphasized in classical theory gave rise to a new organizational theory, the humanistic (also known as the behavioral or neoclassical) theory

  2. Much of humanistic organizational theory grew out of the Hawthorne experiment, a study done between 1927 and 1933 by researchers from Harvard University

    a. The Hawthorne experiment studied certain aspects of classical organizational theory, in particular, the relationship between working conditions and worker productivity

   b. The researchers discovered that various psychological and social factors in the work situation exert more influence on productivity than do actual physical conditions; this is known as the *Hawthorne effect*

   c. The Hawthorne experiment altered the course of organizational study and moved it toward the exploration of the social climate of organizations, the so-called "informal" organizational structures

B. Key concepts

   1. Humanistic organizational theory is concerned with formal and informal organizational structures and with the people working within the organization

   2. Humanistic organizational theory focuses on group productivity, rather than on individual productivity, and on the factors that increase or decrease it

   3. Central premises of humanistic organizational theory are that increased worker morale results in increased productivity; that morale and thus productivity are directly related to the social environment of the work group; and that productivity is related not only to monetary rewards but also to psychological rewards, such as group membership, a sense of belonging, and cohesion

   4. Humanistic organizational theory led the way for the study of informal and formal organizational structures

C. Applications to nursing

   1. The staff nurse must understand both the informal and the formal structure of the health care organization

   2. A nurse manager's fostering of group cohesion and loyalty encourages nurses to work to capacity even when the work environment is less than ideal

   3. Encouraging staff nurse participation in planning and decision making improves morale and increases productivity

   4. A health care organization follows humanistic principles when it addresses employees' social needs by providing nonmonetary rewards such as health benefits and on-site child care

   5. The primary client care delivery system (see Section II. E in Chapter 4) is based on humanistic organizational theory

IV. Modern organizational theory

A. General information

   1. Questions about aspects of the classical and humanistic organizational theories led to the development of a more modern organizational theory

   2. Researchers from various disciplines have contributed to modern organizational theory

3. Development of modern organizational theory began in the 1960s, and it continues to evolve today
4. As a result of this continuing evolution, modern organizational theory takes many forms, including matrix theory, organic theory, technologic theory, decision theory, and information-processing theory
5. Regardless of which form the theory takes, all can be subsumed under a *systems framework*, the hallmark of modern organizational theory

B. Key concepts
   1. Modern organizational theory views organizations as complex, dynamic, social systems in which individuals, structure, end products, and environment all contribute to organizational success
     a. This theory views organizations as dynamic, open structures
     b. This view of organizations differs from the classical and humanistic view of organizations as static, closed structures to be analyzed
   2. Modern organizational theory focuses on organizational processes rather than on structure; these processes include INPUT, THROUGHPUT, OUTPUT, and FEEDBACK
   3. This theory highlights the interrelatedness of all parts of an organization and emphasizes the need for communication and cooperation among all parts
   4. The theory is concerned with the development of flexible individual roles and relationships within the organizational structure
   5. Under this theory, the role of management is to monitor and coordinate communication so as to involve all parts of the system in input, throughput, output, and feedback

C. Applications to nursing
   1. Few health care organizations are organized according to principles of modern organizational theory
   2. When working within a systems framework, nurses are directly responsible for planning, implementing, and evaluating all the functions of input, throughput, and output for their clients
   3. Nurses also must communicate to society what nurses are, what they do, why their cost is justified, and why clients need their services
   4. Nurses must be comfortable with the concepts of role flexibility and communication expertise to facilitate achievement of organizational goals

Points to remember

The classical school of organizational theory represents the earliest attempt to study organizations scientifically.

Classical organizational theory is based on the bureaucratic model.

Humanistic organizational theory focuses on formal and informal organizational structures.

Modern organizational theory views organizations as complex, dynamic systems in which individuals, structure, end products, and environment all contribute to organizational success.

Health care organizations may be structured on various principles of organizational theory.

Most hospitals are structured mainly on principles of classical organizational theory.

Glossary

The following terms are defined in Appendix A, page 110.

bureaucracy

feedback

input

output

throughput

Study questions

To evaluate your understanding of this chapter, answer the following questions in the space provided; then compare your responses with the correct answers in Appendix B, page 115.

1. What are three key elements of a bureaucracy? _____

_____

_____

2. What is meant by the Hawthorne experiment? _____

_____

_____

3. What is considered to be the hallmark of modern organizational theory?

_____

_____

4. What is the focus of modern organizational theory? _____

_____

_____

CHAPTER 3

Organizational Structures

Learning objectives

Check off the following items once you've mastered them:

☐ Describe formal and informal organizational structures.

☐ Identify the four types of formal organizational structures.

☐ Describe the differences between centralized and decentralized structures.

☐ Discuss how dual structure affects nursing practice.

☐ Discuss the different types of health care organizations and the settings in which they occur.

I. Introduction

A. An ORGANIZATION is a group of people working together, under formal and informal rules of behavior, to achieve a common purpose

B. Organization also refers to the procedures, polices, and methods involved in achieving this common purpose

C. Thus, organization is both a *structure* and a *process*
   1. Organizational structure refers to the lines of authority, communication, and delegation; it can be formal or informal
   2. Organizational process refers to the methods used to achieve organizational goals

D. An organization's *formal structure* is depicted in its organizational chart
   1. The organizational chart provides a blueprint depicting formal relationships, functions, and activities
   2. In the chart, the organizational structure typically is presented in pyramid form, with each level of rank subordinate to the one above it
   3. The chart designates the levels of management in an organization
   4. It depicts only the salaried employees of that organization

E. An organization defines its goals and purpose in a philosophy or mission statement; this philosophy forms the basis of the formal organizational structure

F. Every organization also has an *informal structure*, characterized by unspoken, often covert, lines of communication and authority relationships not depicted in the organizational chart
   1. The informal structure develops to meet individuals' needs for friendship, a sense of belonging, and power
   2. The lines of communication in the informal structure (commonly called "the grapevine") are concerned mainly with social issues
   3. Persons with access to vital information can become powerful in the informal structure

G. Organizations also possess a unique culture of shared symbols, language, and meaning
   1. Although the organizational chart may contribute to the culture, more often, the informal, unwritten norms and values of an institution shape the culture
   2. Organizational culture encompasses both explicit and implicit expectations for standards of behavior in the workplace
   3. Organizational culture includes the sum total of the shared values and beliefs of an organization that are passed on to newcomers in the form of myths, legends, rituals, and ceremonies

H. The organizational climate, which differs from the culture, refers to how employees perceive the workplace
1. Employee perceptions about the workplace should be consistent with the organizational culture
2. If perceptions do not mesh with the culture, the organizational climate will be perceived as nonsupportive and unorganized

I. The structure of a health care organization is relevant to the practice of nursing
1. Like any organization, a health care institution has a formal and an informal organizational structure
2. An institution's nursing department usually is structured much like the institution's overall organizational structure
3. An institution's organizational chart depicts how the nursing department fits into the organizational structure and indicates the status and accountability of nurses within the organization
4. Understanding the organizational structure helps the nurse learn the roles, relationships, and lines of communication in the institution
5. Understanding the organizational culture helps the nurse expand knowledge of the norms and values of various institutions
6. Assessment of an organization's climate helps the nurse evaluate the attractiveness of the workplace
7. Understanding the organizational process, including the institution's and the nursing department's philosophy, helps the nurse identify ways to achieve personal and organizational goals

II. Types of formal organizational structure

A. General information
1. Every organization creates a formal structure, which depicts lines of authority and communication and directs organizational goal attainment
2. This formal organizational structure provides a framework for defining responsibility, authority, delegation, and accountability
3. Depending on the organizational philosophy, the formal structure may be rigid or loose

B. Bureaucratic structure
1. Bureaucratic structure is the predominant type of organizational structure in health care institutions
2. This structure is characterized by many hierarchical levels and specialized positions
3. Each level has a specific, clearly defined set of rules and regulations and scope of authority and accountability
4. Each person at a particular level is directly responsible to an immediate supervisor

C. Functionalized structure

    1. Functionalized structure is characterized by persons in specialized advisory or STAFF POSITIONS

    2. These specialists enhance managerial functions by providing information and expertise to the employees of an organization but have no authority to enforce decisions

D. Ad hoc structure

    1. Ad hoc structure is characterized by a more open, flexible operational mode

    2. Teams are created by top-level management for a specific purpose, such as a goal or task

       a. These teams are supplementary and temporary

       b. They operate within the formal structure as a separate entity, depicted in the organizational chart as horizontally attached to the structure

       c. The teams give advice and coordinate the work of the organization

E. Matrix structure

    1. Matrix structure is characterized by teams built directly into the organizational structure

       a. These teams are coordinated both vertically (within the hierarchy) and horizontally (among the groups involved)

       b. The team has formal authority to make and enforce decisions

    2. Matrix structure usually involves less rigid adherence to rules and procedures

F. Applications to nursing

    1. The organizational structure, as depicted in the organizational chart, provides information about status and authority relationships for the nurse

    2. The placement of nursing in the organizational chart depicts nursing's status within that organization

    3. Placement involves both the number and the nature of the hierarchical levels between the nursing department and the executive or top level; for example, in an organization that gives nursing a high status, the top nurse executive may be directly accountable to the chief executive officer (CEO)

III. Forms of organizational structure

A. General information

    1. An organization selects a structural form that best fits its organizational philosophy

    2. Organizational structures take two basic forms: CENTRALIZED and DECENTRALIZED STRUCTURES

    3. Depending on the structural form, the organizational chart depicts the organizational structure as a tall, pyramidal model or a flat, matrix model

4. In both centralized and decentralized structures, the organizational chart delineates LINE POSITIONS, *staff positions*, and SPAN OF CONTROL
5. The number of management levels and the extent of span of control indicate the degree of centralization within an organization
6. Line positions refer to the formal lines of communication and authority depicted in an organizational chart by solid vertical and horizontal lines
   a. *Vertical* line positions extend from the CEO or other top official to the staff at the bottom, denoting the official chain of command
      (1) Vertical structures will diminish in height as computer information systems render them obsolete
      (2) Diversifying into new markets through the addition of services and buildings is called *vertical integration;* its purpose is to increase financial stability
      (3) Vertical management attempts to limit decentralized decision-making by obtaining input from other organizational levels only on single issues of major importance
   b. *Horizontal* line positions depict the division of labor among persons with similar authority and responsibility but different functions
      (1) Merging with pre-existing hospitals and health care institutions to consolidate operations is called *horizontal integration;* its purpose is to reduce operating costs
      (2) Horizontal management attempts to improve communication and decision making by obtaining input from departments that traditionally have been viewed as separate entities
7. Staff positions refer to persons employed by an organization to provide advisory assistance and expertise; these positions are depicted in the organizational chart by dotted lines
   a. Staff positions are used to enhance managerial activity
   b. Persons in staff positions have no decision-making authority
8. Span of control refers to the number of employees a manager can effectively oversee

B. Centralized structure
1. In a centralized structure, power and authority are concentrated in relatively few persons or positions (see *A Centralized Organization)*
2. A centralized structure has many levels or departments, each one highly specialized and subject to rigid rules and procedures
3. In a centralized structure, with its rigid rules and procedures, spans of control are short and employees and managers are in close contact
4. A centralized structure generates a tall, pyramid-shaped organizational chart depicting the multileveled hierarchy of management and individual managers' short spans of control
5. The many levels of a typical centralized structure may cause communication problems within the organization

A CENTRALIZED ORGANIZATION

This organizational chart shows a centralized nursing department and its hierarchical relationship to hospital administration. Its structure centralizes decision-making power and authority in the hands of a few people.

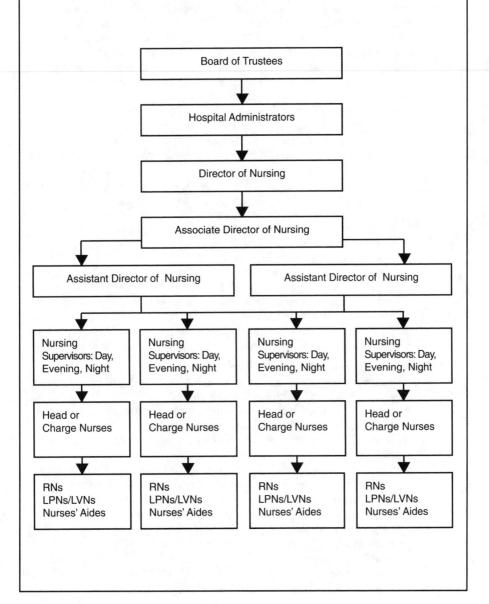

6. In a centralized structure, leaders and managers tend to function in an autocratic management style, demanding rigid adherence to rules and procedures

C. Decentralized structure
   1. In a decentralized structure, power and authority are shifted from the hands of a few persons at the top of the organizational structure to subordinate hierarchical levels
   2. This structure promotes independence, responsibility, and quicker decision making at all levels of an organization
   3. A decentralized structure generates a flat or matrix organizational chart, which depicts fewer management levels and wider spans of control than seen in a centralized structure
   4. This wide span of control means that employees and managers have less contact with each other than in a centralized structure
   5. A decentralized structure has fewer hierarchical levels than a centralized structure and tends to have better communication among levels
   6. In a decentralized structure, leaders and managers tend to function democratically
      a. Managers act as resource persons rather than as authority figures
      b. Employees function more autonomously, with greater responsibility and accountability
   7. Autonomy and a sense of empowerment pervade some decentralized health care institutions; as a result of their attractiveness to employees, these institutions have been labeled "magnet hospitals"
      a. Magnet hospitals embody a culture of excellence demonstrated by an atmosphere of collaboration and trust
      b. Along with decentralization, magnet hospitals use flexible models of nursing care delivery systems (see *A Decentralized Organization*)

D. Applications to nursing
   1. A nursing unit often is a decentralized structure operating within an overall centralized health care organization
   2. A highly centralized structure usually limits the degree of autonomy and authority available to nurses
   3. Bureaucratic structures remain a chief cause of job dissatisfaction among nurses
      a. To enhance nurses' job satisfaction, some health care organizations have attempted to decentralize the organizational structure by giving nurses more control over their work environment
      b. However, a shortage of nursing personnel is causing many health care organizations to return to more centralized structures, which may result in greater consumer dissatisfaction with the delivery of health care services
   4. Cost-containment concerns have led many health care organizations to decrease both line and staff positions

A DECENTRALIZED ORGANIZATION

This organizational chart shows a decentralized nursing department and its hierarchical relationships to hospital administration. Its structure decentralizes decision-making power and authority and places it in the hands of several directors.

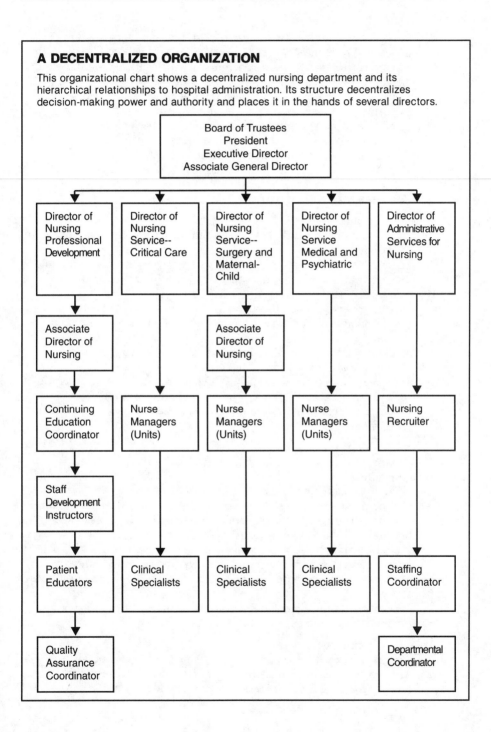

5. Health care organizations are unique in that they employ a dual structure for the medical staff, in which certain private physicians are authorized to practice within the organization but are not salaried and therefore not depicted in the organizational chart
   a. Physicians in this capacity have vertical as well as horizontal line positions; nurses are directly accountable to the organizational hierarchy but also must comply with the physician's orders
   b. An awareness of this dual structure in most health care organizations can help nurses identify potential conflicts in authority and accountability issues and take steps to avoid them

IV. Types of health care organizations

A. General information
   1. The national health care delivery system includes many types of health care organizations
   2. These health care organizations use various procedures, policies, and methods to achieve a common primary goal—to serve the public's health care needs
      a. This goal is achieved through administration of client care, education of health care personnel and the public, research, and health promotion
      b. Other goals of a health care organization may vary, depending on the type and philosophy of the organization
   3. Most health care organizations are formal, centralized, bureaucratic structures with definite lines of authority and communication
   4. Health care organizations often are categorized by their major source of funding

B. Official health care organizations
   1. Organized according to mandates from local, state, or federal government
   2. Funded through governmental budgetary allocations
   3. Can occur at the local, state, or federal levels and include city, county, and state health departments; state hospitals; the U.S. Public Health Service; and the National Institutes of Health
   4. Provide health-related and social welfare services, public works, police and fire services, agricultural services, and housing assistance
   5. Coordinate those activities best accomplished through community-wide action
   6. Typically are centralized bureaucratic structures but can also be functionalized, ad hoc, or matrix structures

C. Voluntary health care organizations
   1. Organized according to policies set by an elected board of trustees
   2. Are *not-for-profit* organizations exempt from federal taxes, with operating costs covered by fees and private endowments

3. Typically started by individuals or groups to address a specific need for service, often focusing on a single group or disease
4. Provide health services to many people in various settings; may augment services provided by official health care organizations
5. Usually include research and educational activities
6. Can occur at the local level (for example, a local visiting nurse association and city or county mental health associations), state level (for example, a state cancer society or state heart association), or national level (for example, the American Diabetes Association and American Red Cross)
7. Can be centralized or decentralized in form
8. May be bureaucratic, functionalized, ad hoc, or matrix in structure

D. Proprietary health care organizations
1. Organized by their owners
2. Provide direct health care services and contribute to health care through the establishment and enforcement of professional practice standards and funding for education and research
3. Funded through third-party payments, fees for services, and membership fees; ineligible for federal tax exemption
4. Include private independent providers such as medical group practices, some hospitals and institutions, and home care agencies
5. May be centralized or decentralized in form and bureaucratic, functionalized, ad hoc, or matrix in structure

E. Applications to nursing
1. Nurses—especially nurse leaders and managers—should be aware of the structure, form, and purpose of their health care organization
2. The nurse leader's or manager's roles and functions may differ depending on the type of health care organization in which he or she works
3. Various degrees of autonomy and responsibility in different types of organizations make role flexibility essential for goal achievement
4. The nurse leader or manager should apply leadership and management principles to function effectively in any type of health care organization

V. Health care settings

A. General information
1. The three basic types of health care organizations include various health care settings
2. Regardless of its organizational structure, form, or type, a health care organization usually is categorized by the setting in which client care is delivered
3. Health care organizations deliver client care in inpatient or outpatient settings

B. Inpatient settings
1. Acute care settings, such as hospitals and trauma centers, represent the majority of inpatient health care settings
2. Long-term care settings are growing in number as the population ages; these settings include skilled nursing facilities, nursing and convalescent homes, and rehabilitation centers

C. Outpatient settings
1. Ambulatory care settings are either hospital- or community-based and include surgicenters, clinics, and physicians' offices
2. Community-care settings, including home-based care, are on the increase, as a result of shorter hospital stays; visiting nurse associations and home health care agencies provide care in these settings

D. Applications to nursing
1. Acute care settings remain the chief source of employment for nurse leaders and managers
2. However, the increasing number of outpatient settings provides nurse leaders and managers with greater opportunities for advancement, growth, and autonomy
3. Nurse leaders and managers need to be aware of the purpose, structure, and form of the setting in which they work to enhance the overall goals of the organization, which will ultimately lead to personal goal achievement and improved client care
4. A nurse leader's or manager's values and beliefs must be consistent with those of the setting in which he or she works to promote personal and job satisfaction and thereby enhance productivity

Points to remember

Organization is both a structure and a process. Organizational structure refers to the lines of authority, communication, and delegation; organizational process refers to the methods used to achieve organizational goals.

An organization's formal structure is depicted in its organizational chart. The organizational chart provides a blueprint of the organization, depicting formal relationships, functions, and activities.

Types of organizational structures include bureaucratic, functionalized, ad hoc, and matrix.

Health care organizations typically are formal, centralized, bureaucratic structures.

Glossary

The following terms are defined in Appendix A, page 110.

centralized structure   organization

decentralized structure   span of control

line position   staff position

Study questions

To evaluate your understanding of this chapter, answer the following questions in the space provided; then compare your responses with the correct answers in Appendix B, page 115.

1. What forms the basis of the formal organizational structure? _____

   _____

   _____

2. What are the two basic forms of organizational structure? _____

   _____

   _____

3. What is meant by organizational climate? _____

   _____

   _____

4. What are three types of health care organizations categorized by their major source of funding? _____

   _____

   _____

CHAPTER 4

Organization and Delivery of Nursing Care

Learning objectives

Check off the following items once you've mastered them:

☐ Identify the major components required to deliver effective nursing care.

☐ Discuss each type of client care delivery system.

☐ Identify the types of client care delivery systems used in centralized and decentralized organizations.

I. Introduction

A. Delivery of nursing care is a means to achieve the goals of the health care organization

B. Effective delivery of nursing care promotes efficiency in an organization through high productivity and adequate STAFFING

C. Effective delivery of nursing care helps increases nurses' job satisfaction

II. Types of client care delivery systems

A. General information
1. Client care delivery refers to the manner in which nursing care is organized and provided
2. Client care delivery is organized at the unit level in much the same way that the nursing department and the health care organization are organized
3. The type of client care delivery system used in a health care organization reflects the organization's philosophy; it also depends on such factors as organizational structure, nurse staffing, and client population

B. Case nursing
1. This is the oldest approach to client care
2. It involves a 1-to-1 nurse-client ratio, with one nurse responsible for caring for one client and providing all the client care required while on duty
3. The responsible nurse reports to a head nurse, charge nurse, or nurse manager
4. Although this approach to client care is expensive, it continues to be used in critical care units (see *Types of Client Care Delivery Systems*, pages 32 and 33)

C. Functional nursing
1. This fragmented approach to care focuses on tasks and procedures and emphasizes efficiency, division of labor, and rigid controls
2. It reflects a bureaucratic, centralized organization
3. Tasks are assigned to various personnel based on complexity and required skill; for example, nursing assistants might bathe clients, practical nurses might provide certain treatments, and registered nurses would administer medications
4. Each staff member is responsible only for assigned tasks while on duty
5. The charge nurse is responsible for coordinating the activities of the unit and reports to the nurse manager; in some cases, a nurse manager may act as the charge nurse
6. Although functional nursing may be useful during times of critical staff shortages, job satisfaction may be reduced because the nurse does not see the effects of total client care

D. Team nursing
1. Organizing client care according to the team nursing approach reflects decentralization at the unit level and an attempt to support goal achievement through group action
2. The TEAM LEADER, rather than the nurse manager, is responsible for managing the care of a group of clients
3. Working with the team leader are various qualified personnel; these personnel report to the team leader, who then reports to the head nurse
4. The team leader assigns personnel based on their qualifications and client needs
5. The team leader is responsible for planning and evaluating the nursing care provided by the team members
6. The nurse manager remains responsible for major management decisions, communication, and coordination for the designated unit or units

E. Primary nursing
1. Primary nursing care reflects a decentralized organizational structure
2. The primary nursing approach is a professional nursing model because it fosters nurses' commitment to and accountability for quality client care
3. A PRIMARY NURSE (an RN) is assigned to care for a group of clients throughout their hospital stays
   a. The primary nurse has 24-hour responsibility for the assigned clients
   b. The primary nurse is responsible for assessing, planning, implementing, and evaluating nursing care
   c. The primary nurse coordinates care through ongoing care plans; ASSOCIATE NURSES carry out the plan of care when the primary nurse is unavailable
4. The nurse manager is responsible for assigning primary nurses, coordinating the activities of primary nurses on all shifts, and assigning associate nurses for periods when primary nurses are off duty

F. Contemporary nursing models
1. In a time of economic uncertainty, health care institutions are becoming consumer driven rather than management driven
2. The contemporary nursing approach views nurses as service providers integral to the success of the organization
3. Newer models of workplace redesign and changing relationships between workers and management reflect this consumer-driven approach

TYPES OF CLIENT CARE DELIVERY SYSTEMS

DELIVERY SYSTEM	DESCRIPTION	ACCOUNTABILITY FOR CLIENT CARE
Case nursing	• Based on holistic philosophy of nursing • Nurse is responsible for care and observation of specific clients • Involves a 1-to-1 nurse-client ratio	• Nurse manager's responsibility
Functional nursing	• Based on task-oriented philosophy of nursing • Nurse performs specific tasks according to charge nurse's schedule	• Charge nurse's responsibility
Team nursing	• Based on group philosophy of nursing • Six or seven professional and nonprofessional personnel staff members work as a team, supervised by a team leader	• Team leader's responsibility
Primary nursing	• Based on comprehensive, personal philosophy of nursing • Nurse is responsible for all aspects of care—from assessing client's condition to coordinating client's care—for specific clients • Involves a 1-to-4 or -5 nurse-client ratio and case-method assignments	• Primary nurse's responsibility

4. Independent work teams, group practice, partnership, PROFESSIONAL PRACTICE, SELF-GOVERNANCE, SHARED GOVERNANCE, stock ownership, and GAINSHARING are just a few of the new approaches that represent attempts to directly involve employees in institutional effectiveness

5. Using primary nursing as a basic structure, *case management* has emerged as a system of client care that focuses on an entire episode of illness across all settings in which the client receives care
   a. The nurse case manager works with case managers in other settings in a group practice structure
   b. The nurse case manager also works with physicians for each particular case type in a joint or collabortive practice structure

6. Using primary nursing, team nursing, functional nursing, or case management as a basic structure, *managed care* emphasizes achievable outcomes, effective use of resources, and cost control at the unit level

ADVANTAGES	DISADVANTAGES
• Improves nurse's responsiveness to client's changing needs • Improves continuity of care • May increase nurse's job satisfaction	• Increases personnel costs
• Reduces personnel costs • Supports cost controls	• Fragments nursing care • May decrease staff job satisfaction • Decreases personal contact with client • Limits continuity of care
• Supports comprehensive care • May increase job satisfaction • Increases cost-effectiveness	• Decreases personal contact with client • Limits continuity of care
• May increase job satisfaction • Improves continuity of care • Allows independent decision making • Supports direct nurse-client communication • Encourages discharge planning • Improves quality of care • May increase cost-effectiveness when comparing nursing assistants' and LPNs' "down time"	• Increases personnel costs initially • Requires properly trained nurses to carry out system's principles • Restricts opportunity for evening- and night-shift nurses to participate

    a. Using various diagnosis-related groups as prototypes, managed care follows a time frame called a critical path; critical paths take into account the usual length of stay, interventions and their timing, resources needed, and expected client outcomes

    b. Managed care also may rely on the use of case management plans; these plans include nursing diagnoses, client outcomes, and the nursing and medical plans of care

  7. Other responses to economic uncertainty and consumer satisfaction have resulted in various forms of differentiated practice

    a. Using primary nursing as a basic structure, ancillary personnel may be employed as nurse extenders who perform client care tasks or clerical tasks under a professional nurse's supervision

    b. Other models of differentiated practice are based on education or assessment

(1) In an educationally based approach, a nurse with a bachelor's degree in nursing is considered the professional and nurses with less education are considered technicians

(2) An assessment-based model differentiates staff according to ability, experience, and expertise

G. Applications to nursing

1. Each client care delivery system has certain advantages and disadvantages

2. The nursing shortage has caused some health care organizations to return to more centralized and bureaucratic client care delivery systems

3. In particular, the functional approach to client care is regaining favor because of its efficiency and comparative low cost

4. The nurse's awareness of the client care delivery system used in various health care organizations helps guide the choice of work environment

5. To survive, health care organizations will be experimenting with new forms of organization and management; nurses must be prepared to contribute to and function in systems that reflect efficiency and quality

Points to remember

Effective delivery of nursing care hinges on an effective client care delivery system and adequate staffing.

Client care delivery systems include case nursing, functional nursing, team nursing, primary nursing, and contemporary nursing models.

Primary nursing reflects a decentralized organizational structure.

Glossary

The following terms are defined in Appendix A, page 110.

associate nurse	self-governance
gainsharing	shared governance
primary nurse	staffing
professional practice	team leader

Study questions

To evaluate your understanding of this chapter, answer the following questions in the space provided; then compare your responses with the correct answers in Appendix B, pages 115 and 116.

1. Which is the oldest type of client care delivery system? _____

_____

_____

2. Which type of client care delivery system reflects a bureaucratic, centralized organization? _____

_____

3. In team nursing, what are the team leader's responsibilities? _____

_____

_____

4. What type of organizational structure is reflected in primary nursing?

_____

_____

5. What is a critical path? _____

_____

CHAPTER 5

Theories of Leadership and Management

Learning objectives

Check off the following items once you've mastered them:

☐ Discuss the theories of leadership.

☐ Compare and contrast the "great man" and trait theories.

☐ List the four elements of situational leadership theory.

☐ Describe the four styles of leadership and management in the tridimensional leadership effectiveness model.

☐ Identify the type of leadership theory likely to be found in a magnet hospital.

I. Introduction

A. Theories of leadership and management attempt to describe and explain who a leader or manager is, what a leader or manager does, and under what conditions or through which behaviors a leader or manager can solve problems and attain goals

B. All leadership and management theories emphasize the relationship aspects and task aspects of the leader and manager roles
   1. Relationship implies a concern for people
   2. Task implies a concern for productivity

II. "Great man" theory

A. Key concepts
   1. The "GREAT MAN" theory is one of the oldest theories of leadership
   2. This theory is based on the belief that a good leader has specific personal characteristics that set him or her apart from others
   3. The "great man" theory posits that certain persons are "born to lead" and that leadership ability is inherited
   4. According to this theory, leadership is an inherent quality and cannot be taught or learned
   5. Also according to this theory, an effective nurse leader in one situation will be an effective leader in any situation; an effective nurse leader exerts control over all aspects of a situation

B. Applications to nursing
   1. According to this theory, a nurse leader attains a position based on innate leadership ability
   2. A "born" nurse leader will be effective in all situations, regardless of internal or external factors

III. Trait theory

A. Key concepts
   1. The TRAIT THEORY is based mainly on the "great man" theory, differing in the position that leadership qualities can be identified and then taught to others
   2. Trait theory identifies personality traits—including intelligence, knowledge, skill, energy and enthusiasm, initiative, self-confidence, patience, persistence, and empathy—considered essential to leadership
   3. The trait theory was the basis for most of the leadership research generated until the 1940s, but has been largely discredited since then
   4. Over the past several decades, the shortcomings of trait theory as the sole explanation of leadership behavior and success have become apparent

5. In practice, various leadership traits have proven difficult to identify clearly and have not been useful in predicting a person's leadership abilities; studies of successful leaders have demonstrated that most had only some of the "essential" leadership traits

B. Applications to nursing
   1. A nurse leader should possess the essential personality traits of leadership
   2. Nursing schools and health care organizations should teach nurses these essential traits

IV. Situational theory

A. Key concepts
   1. SITUATIONAL THEORY expands on trait theory, holding that the essential traits for a leader vary and are determined by a particular situation
   2. Based on the situation, an effective leader adopts an appropriate leadership style that emphasizes certain traits and deemphasizes others
   3. First proposed in the late 1930s, situational theory led researchers to explore the settings in which leadership occurs
   4. Situational theory considers four basic elements of a situation: the *organization* (size, structure, and purpose), the *climate* (atmosphere of the organization, either supportive or nonsupportive), *leader characteristics* (power, authority, and influence), and *follower characteristics* (knowledge, dedication, and tolerance for ambiguity)
   5. The leader analyzes these four elements in a given situation and chooses an appropriate leadership style
   6. Appropriate leadership styles include autocratic, democratic, laissez-faire, or a combination of these styles
   7. Group performance depends on the leader choosing an appropriate leadership style

B. Applications to nursing
   1. An effective nurse leader will combine the best points of the three traditional leadership styles—autocratic, democratic, and laissez-faire—and, depending on the situation, use elements of all three; this approach is called a *multicratic* leadership style
   2. The style used in a particular situation should be based on an analysis of the four elements of situational theory: the organization, climate, leader characteristics, and follower characteristics
   3. In a crisis situation or a situation in which the followers have little or no knowledge or experience, an autocratic style of leadership may be appropriate; for example, during a code situation for a client with cardiac arrest, the leader takes total control, issues directives, and excludes group decision making

    4. A situation requiring group input and group cooperation may call for a democratic leadership style: for example, if a nursing unit adopts a new method of charting, the leader allows for group input to involve group members and encourage success

    5. In a situation in which the followers are highly motivated, self-directed professionals who need little supervision, a laissez-faire leadership style may be most appropriate

V. Interactional theory

A. Key concepts

    1. The "great man," trait, and situational leadership theories do not predict which kinds of leadership behaviors will be most effective under specific circumstances

    2. A concern for measuring leadership effectiveness spawned a new approach to the study of leadership, called the INTERACTIONAL THEORY

    3. Because this theory equates leadership effectiveness with high group work performance, it acts as a theory of leadership and management

    4. One of the most useful interactional models for nursing is the *tridimensional leadership effectiveness model* developed by Paul Hersey and Kenneth Blanchard, which focuses on three areas: leader behavior, group maturity, and leader effectiveness

       a. *Leader behavior* refers to various combinations of task or directing versus relationship or supporting behaviors

       b. *Group maturity* refers to both psychological and job maturity and involves commitment (defined as confidence and motivation) and competence (defined as knowledge and technical skill) to perform required tasks; the tridimensional leadership effectiveness model holds that leader behavior should be based on group maturity

       c. *Leader effectiveness* is measured by the *leader effectiveness and adaptability description (LEAD)*, which includes the leader's perceptions (LEAD-self) and the group members' perceptions (LEAD-other) of the leader's style, flexibility, and overall effectiveness

    5. Four leader behaviors may be used: *directing behavior* is appropriate for a group member with low competence and high commitment; *coaching behavior*, for a group member with some competence and low commitment; *supporting behavior*, for a group member with high competence and variable commitment; and *delegating behavior*, for a group member with high competence and high commitment

    6. According to the tridimensional leadership effectiveness model, leadership effectiveness hinges on choosing and implementing a leadership style appropriate to the task, situation, and level of group maturity

7. Four basic leadership styles emerge from this model: *high directive and low supportive*, characterized as directing behavior in which the leader closely supervises task accomplishment; *high directive and high supportive*, characterized as coaching behavior in which the leader closely supervises task accomplishment and also supports performance through praise, listening, and facilitating; *high supportive and low directive*, characterized as supporting behavior in which the leader facilitates and encourages group members' progress toward task accomplishment; and *low supportive and low directive*, characterized as delegating behavior in which the leader allows group members to make their own decisions

B. Applications to nursing
   1. Interactional theory suggests that an effective nurse leader must adopt a leadership style based on accurate assessment of group maturity
   2. Leader behaviors—directing, coaching, supporting, and delegating—are required of all nurses; thus, all nurses have the potential to become effective leaders
   3. The nurse leader adopts one of four basic leadership styles—high directive and low supportive, high directive and high supportive, high supportive and low directive, or low supportive and low directive—at the unit and overall health care organization levels, depending on the situation, to enhance group performance

VI. Transformational theory

A. Key concepts
   1. In today's rapidly changing health care system, leaders are called on to positively influence both their followers and their organizations
   2. According to TRANSFORMATIONAL THEORY, leaders build trust and self-esteem in themselves and others
   3. A transformational leader attempts to create a workplace that is meaningful, inspiring, and motivational
   4. Transformational leadership results in a workplace with a shared culture of committment to excellence and mutual growth
   5. Transformational theory is most likely to be applied in magnet hospitals

B. Applications to nursing
   1. Transformational leadership is seen in health care organizations with a commitment to excellence
      a. In these organizations, nurses are rewarded for advanced and continuing education, certification status, and clinical excellence
      b. Nurses receive a yearly salary rather than an hourly wage
      c. Accountability for practice is the hallmark of these organizations
   2. Decentralized organizations are crucial for the development of transformational leaders
   3. Decision making and communication are shared equally in institutions that support transformational leadership

Points to remember

Leadership and management theories share a common emphasis on task and relationship aspects of the leader's and manager's roles.

An effective leadership style is flexible and based on the task, the situation, and the level of group maturity.

In a crisis situation, an autocratic leadership style may be most effective.

When time allows discussion and group input, a democratic leadership style may be most effective.

In a group composed of highly motivated, independent members, a laissez-faire leadership style may be most effective.

Glossary

The following terms are defined in Appendix A, page 110.

"great man" theory

interactional theory

situational theory

trait theory

transformational theory

Study questions

To evaluate your understanding of this chapter, answer the following questions in the space provided; then compare your responses with the correct answers in Appendix B, page 116.

1. How does the "great man" theory attempt to explain leadership? _____

   _____

   _____

2. How does the trait theory attempt to explain leadership? _____

   _____

   _____

3. According to the situational theory, on what does group performance

   depend? _____ _____

   _____

4. On what three areas does the tridimensional leadership effectiveness model

   focus? _____

   _____

5. What type of workplace is created by transformational leadership? _____

   _____

   _____

CHAPTER 6

Concepts in Leadership and Management

Learning objectives

Check off the following items once you've mastered them:

☐ Discuss the force field model of change.

☐ Describe the various phases of conflict.

☐ Differentiate between group process and group dynamics.

☐ Identify the components of upward, downward, and lateral communication.

☐ Discuss the different sources of power.

☐ Describe the role of politics in organizations.

☐ List the steps in decision making.

I. Introduction

A. The concepts used in leadership and management are derived from abstract ways of looking at certain issues

B. These concepts serve as guidelines and provide a framework for addressing the essential issues of leadership and management

C. Some concepts have resulted in models that clarify the issues

D. These concepts help apply the theories of organization, leadership, and management to nursing practice

II. Change

A. Key concepts
1. Change is a constant in today's health care organizations
2. Various economic, demographic, and technologic forces spur widespread and varied changes in health care
3. These changes may be planned or unplanned
   a. *Planned* change is an active process involving predetermined goals, participative management, a change agent, and a target for change
   b. *Unplanned change* is a reactive process whereby change either occurs without personal involvement or is introduced by outside forces
4. Planned change is initiated and guided by a skilled professional or a change agent; the change agent may be internal or external to the organization
5. The target for change may involve policies or procedures (first-order change); most change also involves the knowledge, behavior, and attitudes of others (second-order change)
6. Kurt Lewin's *force field model of change*, developed in 1951, provides a dynamic, theoretical view of the change process
   a. According to Lewin's model, in every situation two forces—DRIVING FORCES and RESTRAINING FORCES—operate in opposition
   b. Driving forces influence movement toward a goal; restraining forces obstruct goal achievement
   c. When driving forces equal restraining forces, the *status quo* is maintained
   d. Changing the status quo involves a conscious effort to increase the driving forces and decrease the restraining forces
   e. Once this occurs, planned change can take place in a three-step process of UNFREEZING, MOVING, and REFREEZING
      (1) During unfreezing, forces emerge that threaten change, a concept known as resistance
      (2) Various strategies for handling resistance have been identified: POWER-COERCIVE, NORMATIVE-REEDUCATIVE, and EMPIRICAL-RATIONAL

7. The key ingredient in change is power

B. Applications to nursing
1. Lewin's force field model of change serves as a nursing management tool
2. Nursing leadership involves initiating changes that will enhance nursing practice
3. Nurses also can act as change agents in efforts to restructure the overall health care delivery system
4. Integral to this nursing role as change agent is the need for a strong power base that provides formal and informal sources of support
5. Nurses must learn to thrive on change and become proactive, encompassing a worldview that emphasizes uncertainty and the need to cooperate with others; this new worldview is called a *paradigm shift*

III. Conflict

A. Key concepts
1. Conflict is as inevitable as change
2. Conflict is not always negative; it can be a powerful impetus for positive change
3. Conflict results from a disparity between real or perceived goals, values, roles, attitudes, or actions of two or more persons or groups
4. It can be competitive or disruptive
   a. Competitive conflict follows basic rules emphasizing winning and is usually not associated with anger and hostility
   b. Disruptive conflict does not follow basic rules and involves activities to reduce, defeat, or eliminate the opponent
5. Conflict may be *individual* (within one person), *interpersonal* (between two or more persons), *intragroup* (within a group), or *intergroup* (between two or more groups)
6. Conflict must be managed at the individual, group, and organizational levels
7. A.C. Filley's model of the conflict process developed in 1976 explains how conflict and conflict resolution occur
8. When conflict occurs, it proceeds through various phases: perceived conflict, felt conflict, manifest conflict, conflict resolution or suppression, and conflict aftermath
   a. *Perceived* and *felt conflict* involve awareness of the conflict and feelings of tension, anxiety, and anger
   b. *Manifest conflict* consists of overt behavior, either constructive or destructive

     c. *Conflict resolution* can take one of three forms: *win-lose*, in which one side dominates the other through superior power; *lose-lose*, involving resolution through avoidance, withdrawal, compromise, or bribery, with an outcome unsatisfactory to both sides; or *win-win*, involving resolution through mutual goal setting and collaboration, with an outcome satisfactory to both sides
     d. *Conflict suppression* involves repression or avoidance of conflict on direction of a higher authority
     e. In *conflict aftermath*, a person or group examines the conflict and its outcome and formulates attitudes to manage future conflicts

B. Applications to nursing
    1. Managing conflict is highly individualized, but skills in this area are critical for nurses
    2. A nurse may be involved in simultaneous conflicts at various levels, such as with a client, staff members, or superiors in the health care organization
    3. The nurse's approach to conflict resolution creates a climate that may be constructive or destructive

IV. Group dynamics

A. Key concepts
    1. A *group* is an association of two or more people in an interdependent relationship with shared purposes and shared awareness
    2. How a group works together to achieve goals is called the *group process*
    3. The specific communication and interaction among group members is called *group dynamics*
    4. Organizations consist of two types of groups: the *formal* or work group, which has a clearly defined task designed to meet organizational goals, and the *informal*, or social group, which meets group members' needs for companionship and friendship
    5. Groups tend to pass through clearly observable phases as they develop
     a. In *dependence* (phase I), the "forming" phase, members are insecure, anxious, and ego-centered; they feel the need for support
     b. In *independence* (phase II), the "storming" phase, members become aware of the rules and roles within the group; competition and conflict are intense; members start to view each other as a group but are still conscious of themselves
     c. In *interdependence* (phase III), the "norming" and "performing" phase, members have a strong group identity and trust and feel a sense of responsibility to and for the group; the group task is defined; rules and roles are clearly established and accepted; and group goals are perceived as more important than individual goals
     d. In *termination* (phase IV), the "adjourning" phase, the group's task has been completed and the members prepare to leave the group

6. Group size is an important factor in organizations
   a. As group size increases, so does the complexity of group dynamics
   b. An ideal work group consists of 8 to 10 members, which promotes member satisfaction and effective group process
7. All groups are guided by *group norms* — a set of overt and covert standards that shape the behavior, attitudes, and perceptions of members
8. Individual group members take on certain roles, which can be categorized as *task* (involving the job at hand and means to accomplish it), *maintenance* (involving aspects of group function), and *individual* (involving personal needs irrelevant and inconducive to group function)
9. Effective groups, both formal and informal, are characterized by strong group cohesion, in which members have a high level of attraction for one another
10. Excessive cohesion may hinder a group's receptivity to different opinions and points of view, resulting in a phenomenon known as *group think* — excessive conformity to group values

B. Applications to nursing
1. Recognizing the formal and informal work groups in the health care organization is essential for effective nursing leadership and management
2. Understanding group process and group dynamics can help a nurse become a more effective group member and group leader
3. The nurse leader is responsible for coordinating formal and informal work groups to accomplish individual and organizational goals
4. Accurate identification of a group's developmental phase can help a nurse leader confront group problems effectively
5. Confrontations should be group-centered rather than individual-centered, because a group tends to function as a whole
6. An effective nurse leader is aware of any hidden agendas — covert, private, deeply felt emotional issues that are often disruptive — that the group or individuals may have

V. Communication

A. Key concepts
1. Communication involves the transmission of verbal and nonverbal messages between a sender and a receiver
   a. The sender *encodes* a message — translates it into words and gestures
   b. The receiver then *decodes* the message — translates it into a response
2. Organizations are systems of overlapping and interdependent groups structured into work, authority, status, and friendship arrangements, each with its own communication styles and rules

3. Organizational communication is a complex process that can be taught and learned
4. The many potential barriers to effective organizational communication include time pressures, environmental interference, lack of information, faulty reasoning, organizational complexity, and selective perception
5. Research has shown that 75% of all management problems result from poor communication
6. Organizational communication can be formal or informal
   a. Formal communication may be upward, downward, or lateral, as depicted in the organizational chart
      (1) *Upward communication* involves messages sent from subordinates to superiors; these messages tend to be screened at various management levels so that much of the original message is lost when it arrives at the top
      (2) *Downward communication* involves messages sent from superiors to subordinates, primarily directive in nature
      (3) *Lateral communication* involves messages sent between personnel or departments on the same level, usually dealing with task coordination
   b. Informal communication (the grapevine) also operates through upward, downward, and lateral channels
      (1) The grapevine serves individual needs for power, personal recognition, and social interaction, and may provide information not available through formal channels
      (2) The grapevine can provide rapid communication, but it also can distort information

B. Applications to nursing
   1. Communication is an essential skill for the nurse manager
   2. Nurses should attempt to overcome barriers to effective communication by establishing excellence in verbal (spoken), nonverbal (gestures and body positions), and written communication
   3. Nurse leaders and managers need to practice and develop active listening skills to enhance communication
   4. A nurse manager should encourage feedback from the receiver of a message to help eliminate distorted communication
   5. The effective nurse manager focuses more on lateral communication than on downward communication
   6. Nurses should always adhere to the formal lines of communication, as depicted in the organizational chart, to communicate within the health care organization
   7. Nurses also should recognize the importance of an organization's informal lines of communication and use them to their best advantage

VI. Power

A. Key concepts
   1. Leadership involves the exercise of power
   2. Power is the ability to affect the attitudes or behaviors of others
   3. Power is closely related to influence, which may be either direct or indirect
      a. *Direct influence* is based on role expectations associated with a given position
      b. *Indirect influence* involves role modeling, advice, guidance, and persuasion
   4. *Legitimate power* derives from a formally designated position of authority
   5. *Referent power* derives from the ability to inspire others' admiration of and identification with the leader
   6. *Expert power* derives from the ability to inspire others based on the leader's knowledge, skill, and expertise
   7. *Reward power* derives from the ability to influence behavior by granting rewards
   8. *Coercive power* derives from the ability to influence behavior by withholding rewards or applying sanctions
   9. Legitimate, reward, and coercive power fall into the realm of management; referent and expert power, into the realm of leadership

B. Applications to nursing
   1. All nurse managers possess some degree of legitimate power—authority to carry out organizational decisions and goals
   2. This authority is supplemented by the nurse manager's power to reward or coerce
   3. Nurse managers become leaders through the development of referent and expert power bases that inspire others' obedience and loyalty
   4. By developing referent and expert power, a nurse leader need not rely on legitimate power
   5. A nurse leader can empower others by sharing power through delegation and participation in decision making; empowerment enhances self-competence and self-esteem
   6. Self-competence, as manifested by clinical expertise, advanced knowledge, and expert clinical judgment, is the ultimate form of power
   7. A nurse manager and nurse leader can use the various sources of power to effect change at the unit, organizational, and professional levels

VII. Politics

A. Key concepts
   1. Politics refers to activities aimed at influencing others in decision making and change

2. Politics also refers to the relationships within an organization — including procedures, values, norms, and acceptable behavior — that determine how a person will act in a given situation

3. Politics is closely associated with power

4. It involves using legitimate power to identify opportunities and take advantage of them

5. Knowledge of the organizational structure, lines of communication, and individual roles and functions is essential to effective politics

6. An organization's politics helps determine appropriate management styles within that organization

7. Because politics is based on power, a person interested in political advancement must identify those people with decision-making power and cultivate relationships with them

8. Because groups can exert more power than individuals, joining or organizing a special interest group can increase a person's base of power and support

9. Joining forces with other groups who share a common interest or goal builds alliances and expands the power base to influence those with decision-making power

10. Recognizing and rewarding those in power lays the groundwork for future assistance

B. Applications to nursing

1. Politics in health care organizations is a means to influence people in power to promote quality client care

2. Nurses and nurse managers can use politics to influence policy on the unit, departmental, organizational, and governmental levels

3. Staff nurses can use politics to influence policy on the unit

4. Nurse managers can use politics to influence departmental and organizational policy

5. Nurses on all levels can use politics for career advancement

6. Membership in state nurses' associations or specialty nursing organizations can help nurses participate in defining and regulating nursing

7. In this time of economic uncertainty, the allocation of scarce resources such as health care and the potential of having to ration health care takes on vast political and ethical dimensions

8. Nurses should be aware of the political and ethical ramifications of meeting not only the health care needs of individuals but also of meeting the health care needs of a society with dwindling resources

VIII. Decision making

A. Key concepts

1. Decision making is a core aspect of management; every action by a leader or group springs from a decision

2. Decision making is a process of scientific problem solving that encompasses change, conflict, group dynamics, and communication
3. Decision making involves six basic steps: identifying a problem, identifying possible solutions to the problem, analyzing the possible consequences of each solution, choosing the best possible solution, implementing the solution, and evaluating the results
   a. Generating possible solutions to a problem ideally involves input from group members and tools such as brainstorming and decision models
   b. Choosing the best possible solution to a problem involves such factors as cost, value, feasibility, acceptability, and risk
   c. Implementing the chosen solution involves planning for contingencies to maximize acceptance of the decision
   d. Evaluating the solution involves comparing the consequences of the decision with original expectations
4. Decision makers can use two basic decision-making strategies: optimizing and "satisficing"
   a. An *optimizing strategy* involves examining all solutions and choosing the one that will result in the best possible outcome
   b. A *"satisficing" strategy* involves choosing a solution that is not ideal but does meet minimal standards of satisfying acceptance
5. Decisions often are made under conditions of uncertainty and risk
   a. *Uncertainty* implies a lack of knowledge about the consequences of a decision
   b. *Risk* implies a lack of control over the consequences
6. Decision making under conditions of uncertainty is more difficult, because the decision maker has no rational basis for choosing one alternative over another

B. Applications to nursing
   1. Decision making is especially important in nursing practice, when decisions often have life-and-death significance
   2. The decision-making process is used by nurses and nurse managers in every facet of practice
   3. Whenever possible, nurse managers should use an optimizing strategy for decision making
   4. When group acceptance is important and sufficient time is available, the nurse manager should involve the group in decision making
   5. The nurse manager uses the formal and informal lines of communication within the organization to gather as much information as possible to ensure optimal decision making

Points to remember

Change may be planned or unplanned.

Conflict can be a powerful impetus for change.

Group dynamics refers to communication and interaction among group members.

Organizational communication channels are formal and informal and operate in upward, downward, and lateral directions.

Politics and power are closely related.

Decision making encompasses change, conflict, group dynamics, and communication and is at the very core of management function.

Glossary

The following terms are defined in Appendix A, page 110.

driving forces	power-coercive strategy
empirical-rational strategy	refreezing
moving	restraining forces
normative-reeducative strategy	unfreezing

Study questions

To evaluate your understanding of this chapter, answer the following questions in the space provided; then compare your responses with the correct answers in Appendix B, page 116.

1. What is the key ingredient in change? _____

_____

_____

2. What are the five phases of conflict? _____

_____

_____

3. What are group norms? _____

_____

_____

4. What types of messages typically are sent with downward communication?

_____

_____

5. What is the ultimate form of power? _____

_____

_____

6. What are two basic decision making strategies? _____

_____

_____

CHAPTER 7

Leadership and Management Methods

Learning objectives

Check off the following items once you've mastered them:

☐ Identify the components of management by objectives.

☐ Discuss motivation as a necessary method for management.

☐ List the assumptions in a Theory X and a Theory Y philosophy of management.

☐ Identify the components of participative management.

☐ Describe the concepts of Total Quality Management.

I. Introduction

A. Leadership and management methods refer to actions taken by a leader or manager that produce a desired outcome

B. In health care organizations, the desired outcome is quality client care and staff productivity

C. Leadership and management methods are a means of influencing staff performance

D. The various methods serve as guidelines for motivating, encouraging, and evaluating staff with the aim of enhancing productivity, job satisfaction, and quality care

II. Managerial grid

A. General information
   1. Developed by Robert Blake and Jane Mouton in 1964, the managerial grid is a widely used managerial training tool
   2. This tool presents alternative managerial methods
   3. Use of the grid helps managers evaluate their managerial styles objectively and identify areas that need improvement (see *Managerial Grid*)

B. Key concepts
   1. Two key dimensions of managerial behavior are depicted on the grid: concern for production on the horizontal axis and concern for people on the vertical axis
   2. In each dimension, the manager's relative level of concern is rated on a scale of 1 to 9
   3. These two dimensions are interdependent; every manager considers both dimensions, although often to varying degrees
   4. Five basic management styles are described at the corners and in the center of the grid

C. Leadership and management styles
   1. *Impoverished management* — rated as 1, 1 — is characterized by minimum concern for both production and people
   2. *Authority-obedience management* — rated as 9, 1 — is characterized by great concern for production but minimum concern for people
   3. *Organization-man management* — rated as 5, 5 — is characterized by moderate concern for both production and people
   4. *Country-club management* — rated as 1, 9 — is characterized by minimum concern for production but great concern for people
   5. *Team management* — rated as 9, 9 — is characterized by great concern for both production and people
   6. Blake and Mouton proposed the team management style as the ideal

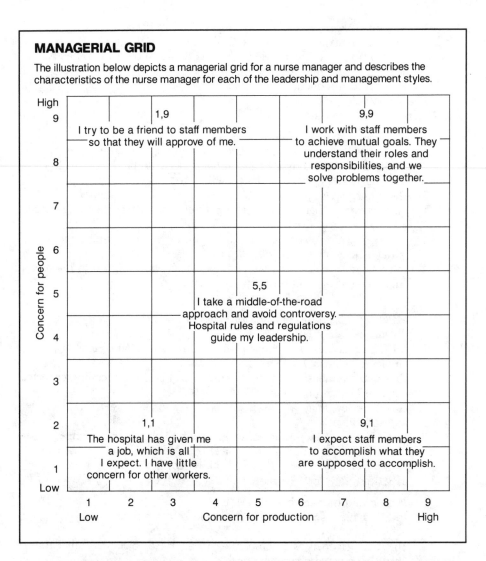

MANAGERIAL GRID

The illustration below depicts a managerial grid for a nurse manager and describes the characteristics of the nurse manager for each of the leadership and management styles.

High
9

1,9
I try to be a friend to staff members so that they will approve of me.

9,9
I work with staff members to achieve mutual goals. They understand their roles and responsibilities, and we solve problems together.

8

7

Concern for people

6

5

5,5
I take a middle-of-the-road approach and avoid controversy. Hospital rules and regulations guide my leadership.

4

3

2

1,1
The hospital has given me a job, which is all I expect. I have little concern for other workers.

9,1
I expect staff members to accomplish what they are supposed to accomplish.

1

Low

1   2   3   4   5   6   7   8   9
Low   Concern for production   High

   a. This style integrates and balances a concern for production and people
   b. Group members feel committed to achieving group goals and individual goals; competition among group members is reduced, and communication and cooperation are enhanced
D. Applications to nursing
   1. The managerial grid provides health care organizations with a means of identifying potential effective nurse managers
   2. Nurse managers can use the managerial grid to assess particular situations and determine the most effective managerial style

3. Nurse managers also can use the grid to identify how their managerial styles fit particular health care organizations
4. The team management style represents the ideal model for effective nursing management; using this approach, a nurse manager integrates concern for production and people

III. Management by objectives

A. General information
  1. Crucial to the management process is planning, which involves decisions about a course of action: what needs to be done, which resources are available, and who will take the necessary action
  2. The management process also involves evaluation, through a mechanism of checks and balances, to ensure control over long-range and short-range plans
  3. Management by objectives (MBO) is both a philosophy and a method of management encompassing planning and evaluation
  4. Introduced by Peter Drucker in 1954, MBO was designed to improve employee morale and productivity

B. Key concepts
  1. MBO provides a mechanism for establishing measurable goals throughout an organization
  2. MBO emphasizes self-control rather than managerial control of employee behavior and stresses teamwork
  3. Employees establish individual standards of performance and expected outcomes based on organizational goals
  4. Goals are formulated at all levels: organizational, departmental, unit, and individual
  5. MBO is a three-step process: writing clear, concise, measurable objectives; developing a plan to meet the objectives; and evaluating the plan at predetermined times and taking corrective action if necessary
  6. MBO results in better organizational planning

C. Leadership and management styles
  1. In MBO, management facilitates employee development and achievement
  2. The manager focuses on employees' measurable objectives rather than on their personal characteristics
  3. The manager is responsible for employee development through setting standards of quality performance, providing well-timed feedback, and giving sufficient rewards
  4. MBO is used less frequently by managers who subscribe to a TOTAL QUALITY MANAGEMENT philosophy (see Section X, page 67)

D. Applications to nursing
   1. Most health care organizations operate under some form of MBO because it provides an effective and consistent method of performance evaluation
   2. Nurses should be aware of their organizational mission, purpose, and goals and their departmental and unit goals when developing their own objectives
   3. MBO places great emphasis on the attributes of values clarification and accountability
   4. In determining plans and aspirations, the nurse manager develops a written list of objectives and priorities and time frames for accomplishing objectives
   5. In this list, objectives should be realistically stated and should encourage personal and professional growth by promoting increased self-awareness, accountability, satisfaction, and productivity

IV. Decision-making models and trees

A. General information
   1. Decision-making models and trees can generate solutions to a problem
   2. Decision-making models use DECISION TREES to solve problems
   3. Decision trees diagram the problem-solving process

B. Key concepts
   1. A decision tree depicts a problem, alternative solutions to the problem, and possible consequences of each solution ranked by the risk or probability of occurrence
   2. The problem must have at least two solutions
   3. As solutions are listed, the decision-making process "branches out" to resemble a tree
   4. Decision-making models include program evaluation and review technique, critical path method, and normative decision making
      a. The *program evaluation and review technique* (PERT) is a network system model of decision making, problem solving, and planning that determines priorities through key activities, time progression, and flow of events
      b. The *critical path method*, an aspect of PERT, diagrams the order in which tasks are to be accomplished or completed
      c. The *Vroom and Yetton normative decision-making model*, developed in 1973, examines specific managerial decision styles
         (1) It examines seven problem attributes: the importance of the quality of the decision, the manager's knowledge or expertise, the group's knowledge or expertise, the problem structure, the importance of the group's acceptance of the decision, the group's acceptance of an autocratic decision, and the group's commitment to organizational goals

    (2) Decision styles are determined by how the seven DECISION RULES apply to a specific situation

    (3) The seven decision rules are the information rule, the goal congruence rule, the unstructured problem rule, the acceptance rule, the conflict rule, the fairness rule, and the acceptance priority rule

C. Leadership and management styles

  1. Vroom and Yetton identified five main managerial decision styles: autocratic I, autocratic II, consultative I, consultative II, and group II

  2. *Autocratic I decision style:* the manager solves the problem or makes the decision using information available only to himself or herself

  3. *Autocratic II decision style:* the manager lacks the information necessary to solve the problem and obtains it from subordinates; the subordinates provide information only about the problem and do not generate or evaluate alternative solutions

  4. *Consultative I decision style:* the manager shares the problem with subordinates individually, then makes a decision that may or may not reflect their input

  5. *Consultative II decision style:* the manager shares the problem with subordinates as a group, then makes a decision that may or may not reflect group input

  6. *Group II decision style:* the manager shares the problem with the group, and together they propose solutions; the manager does not try to influence the group and is willing to implement any solution supported by the group even if it is not the manager's chosen solution (see *Decision Rules and Decision Styles*)

D. Applications to nursing

  1. Decision-making models and trees provide the nurse manager with a quick and effective means of decision making

  2. A nurse manager can use this method of problem solving at the unit and organizational levels

  3. A nurse manager should carefully assess a problem and consult with staff members to determine the most effective solution

  4. A nurse manager must examine an alternative solution's possible consequences and risks carefully to ensure that the decision minimizes loss and maximizes gain

  5. A nurse manager who is aware of organizational and unit objectives can solve problems effectively

V. Motivation

A. General information

  1. To achieve established goals, persons must be motivated

  2. Motivated behavior is goal-directed behavior

  3. Motivating employees to achieve goals is a crucial managerial skill

DECISION RULES AND DECISION STYLES

This chart lists the seven decision rules of the Vroom and Yetton decision-making model and describes them in terms of problem attributes. It then identifies possible decision styles based on the decision rules and problem attributes.

DECISION RULE	PROBLEM ATTRIBUTES CONSIDERED	POSSIBLE DECISION STYLES
Information rule	• Quality of decision is important • Manager lacks information to solve the problem	Autocratic II, Consultative I, Consultative II, Group II
Goal congruence rule	• Quality of decision is important • Subordinates lack shared commitment to organizational goals	Autocratic I, Autocratic II, Consultative I, Consultative II
Unstructured problem rule	• Quality of decision is important • Leader lacks information to solve problem • Problem lacks structure • Interaction among subordinates is important	Consultative II, Group II
Acceptance rule	• Subordinate acceptance is important • Autocratic decision is unacceptable • Subordinate participation is important	Consultative I, Consultative II, Group II
Conflict rule	• Subordinate acceptance is important • Autocratic decision is unacceptable • Subordinates are likely to disagree over decision	Consultative II, Group II
Fairness rule	• Quality of decision is unimportant • Subordinate acceptance is important to implement decision • Autocratic decision is unacceptable	Group II
Acceptance priority rule	• Subordinate acceptance is important to implement decision • Autocratic decision may not be acceptable • Subordinates are allowed to participate in decision making	Group II

4. The Hawthorne experiment (see Section III. A in Chapter 2) ushered in a new era of management that focused on concern for production and employees
5. Subsequent research into MOTIVATION resulted in motivational theories; major motivational theorists include Abraham Maslow, David McClelland, and Frederick Herzberg

B. Key concepts
1. All motivational theories have common threads: concern for what causes human behavior, what directs behavior toward goal accomplishment, and what encourages this behavior over time
2. Maslow described motivation as the innate impetus to satisfy what he termed the hierarchy of human needs: biologic needs, safety needs, need for love and sense of belonging, need for self-esteem, and need for self-actualization
3. McClelland, elaborating on Maslow's hierarchy, identified three motivational needs present in varying degrees in all persons operating in an organizational setting: achievement, affiliation, and control
4. Herzberg's two-factor theory discusses motivation in terms of job satisfaction
   a. The lack of such external factors as adequate salary, job security, and decent working conditions leads to job dissatisfaction and poor work performance
   b. Job satisfaction results mainly from promoting internal factors such as recognition, respect, authority, and status

C. Leadership and management styles
1. The effective motivational manager diagnoses human needs
2. The manager must also diagnose situations, because human needs (and thus the optimal motivational strategy) vary in different situations
3. Motivating employees depends not only on satisfying needs for a safe and secure environment but also on satisfying needs for self-esteem, self-actualization, and achievement
4. The manager recognizes competent work by providing objective feedback and recognition for performance, which motivate continued productivity

D. Applications to nursing
1. Health care organizations use motivation to achieve organizational goals
2. Nurse managers use motivation in daily practice
3. Nurse managers use motivational strategies when leading a team or caring for a group of clients
4. To motivate people, nurse managers must identify their own needs and expectations
5. Nurse managers should set reasonable work goals and reward staff for work well done
   a. A motivated work group has a clear definition of tasks and promotes a friendly, supportive atmosphere

   b. Staff must be challenged to develop expertise and pride in their work

VI. Path-goal theory

A. General information
  1. Robert House's path-goal theory, introduced in 1971, is concerned with motivation and productivity
  2. It attempts to evaluate the effect of the leader on group members
  3. According to this theory, the motivational function of management is to help employees see the relationship between personal and organizational goals, clarify the "paths" to accomplishing these goals, remove obstacles to goal achievement, and reward employees for work accomplished

B. Key concepts
  1. According to this theory, an effective leader or manager clarifies the path to the goal by structuring the work through planning, organizing, directing, and controlling
  2. Structuring the work increases employee productivity
  3. The manager who shows considerate behavior toward employees, engaging in supportive, warm, and friendly relationships with them, helps promote employees' job satisfaction

C. Leadership and management styles
  1. An effective leader or manager adopts a specific behavioral style to increase employee motivation and productivity
  2. *Supportive behavior* considers the needs of employees and fosters a friendly work environment
  3. *Directive behavior* clarifies the path to the goal by structuring the necessary tasks
  4. *Achievement-oriented behavior* challenges employees to strive for excellence
  5. *Participative behavior* engages employees in decision making

D. Applications to nursing
  1. A nurse manager's supportive behavior is especially important for employees engaged in routine nursing tasks
  2. A nurse manager can use directive behavior to demonstrate the relationship between performance and reward and thus improve employee motivation
  3. A nurse manager can use achievement-oriented behavior to challenge staff members to attain excellence in job performance
  4. A nurse manager can use participative behavior to obtain staff input and cooperation in making decisions about goals and how they are to be accomplished

VII. Theory X and Theory Y

A. General information
   1. The directing and evaluating functions of management are shaped by managers' assumptions about their employees
   2. Douglas McGregor, in 1960, labeled these assumptions Theory X and Theory Y
   3. Depending on which set of assumptions the manager subscribes to, the amount of direction and control given to employees will vary

B. Key concepts
   1. *Theory X* assumes that people dislike work and must be directed, controlled, and coerced into working productively; that people will resist authority and responsibility; and that they work only for security and economic rewards
   2. A Theory X–oriented manager emphasizes organizational goals
   3. *Theory Y* assumes that people are creative and imaginative and will achieve satisfaction from work and that people are self-directed and self-controlled and will accept responsibility under favorable conditions
   4. A Theory Y–oriented manager emphasizes individual goals
   5. McGregor believed that each approach is ineffective by itself and, as such, recommended a restructuring of the workplace so that true collaboration can occur while meeting individual goals and working toward organizational goals

C. Leadership and management styles
   1. According to Theory X, a manager should be autocratic, directive, and task-oriented and solicit little input from subordinates
   2. According to Theory Y, a manager should be democratic, supportive, and relationship-oriented and should delegate to and accept input from subordinates

D. Applications to nursing
   1. A nurse manager with a Theory X orientation will allow for minimal employee input, delegate little, supervise closely, and comply strictly with rules and regulations
   2. A nurse manager with a Theory Y orientation will encourage employee input, provide loose supervision, delegate responsibilities, and allow for personal expression

VIII. Contingency model

A. General information
   1. Introduced by Fred Fiedler in 1967, the contingency model of managerial effectiveness is based on group productivity
   2. Although this is a management model, it uses the terms *leader* and *leadership*

3. The leader has primary responsibility for the group and has the power and influence to ensure that the group works effectively
4. Defining leadership as a relationship involving power and influence, Fiedler explored how much power and influence situations provide the leader
5. The contingency model highlights the need for flexibility in leadership behaviors
6. The validity of the contingency model has been supported by effective research

B. Key concepts
1. In the contingency model, three situational variables are used to predict the favorability of a situation for the leader: the leader's interpersonal relations with group members, the leader's LEGITIMATE POWER, and the task structure
2. These three variables produce eight situations ranked from "most favorable" to "least favorable" in terms of their effect on the leader; each of these eight situations is numbered and referred to as a cell
3. Cells 1, 2, 3, and 8 are the most favorable and least favorable situations for the leader, calling for a controlling, autocratic leadership style; cells 4 and 5 are moderately favorable situations, calling for a permissive, democratic leadership style; and cells 6 and 7 are unfavorable situations calling for either a permissive or controlling leadership style

C. Leadership and management styles
1. When relationships with the group are good, the work is structured, and the leader is powerful (cell 1), a task-oriented style is best
2. When relationships with the group are good, the work is structured, and the leader has weak power (cell 2), a task-oriented style is best
3. When relationships with the group are good, the work is unstructured, and the leader is powerful (cell 3), a task-oriented style is best
4. When relationships with the group are poor, the work is unstructured, and the leader has weak power (cell 8), a task-oriented style is best
5. When relationships with the group are good, the work is unstructured, and the leader has weak power (cell 4), a relationship-oriented style is best
6. When relationships with the group are poor, the work is structured, and the leader is powerful (cell 5), a relationship-oriented style is best
7. When relationships with the group are poor, the work is structured, and the leader has weak power (cell 6), a relationship-oriented style is best
8. When relationships with the group are poor, the work is unstructured, and the leader is powerful (cell 7), a relationship-oriented style is best

D. Applications to nursing
  1. According to the contingency model, a nurse manager should modify situations based on group relations, personal power, and task structure to improve staff productivity
  2. A nurse manager who uses the contingency model must have a thorough understanding of his or her relationship with staff members, his or her power and status within the organization, and the nature of the group task
  3. Based on this assessment, the nurse manager can describe the situation as favorable, moderately favorable, or unfavorable
     a. In favorable and unfavorable situations, the nurse manager should adopt a task-oriented approach
     b. In moderately favorable situations, a relationship-oriented approach is best

IX. Participative approach to management (Theory Z)

A. General information
  1. Participative management involves a collaborative approach
  2. William Ouchi's Theory Z, introduced in 1981, is one form of participative management that focuses on ways to motivate workers and thereby increase employee job satisfaction and improve productivity
  3. Participative management combines the elements of MBO, motivational principles, and employee enhancement
  4. Participative management is based on identification of organizational structure and policies, employees' needs and motivations, and measurements of productivity
  5. Participative management integrates the formal and informal structures of the organization through shared goal setting

B. Key concepts
  1. Overall organizational goals are set by top management
  2. Groups involved in participative management have an appointed leader
  3. The leader is granted authority for problems falling under his or her jurisdiction
  4. Participative management is characterized by "quality circles," which involve group decision making
  5. In participative management, decentralized organizational structure, MBO, and group decision making effectively transfer power to the level at which individual decisions must be made
  6. Working under a system of participative management requires shared authority, responsibility, and accountability
  7. The success of participative management hinges on managers' and employees' commitment to the organization

C. Leadership and management styles
   1. Participative management requires that managers have good leadership qualities, because it integrates leadership and management
   2. It promotes a relationship-oriented, democratic leadership style
   3. The leader supports employee achievement and relies on delegating and supporting leadership styles

D. Applications to nursing
   1. Participative management provides a professional model for nursing care
   2. Primary nursing is an essential component of participative management
   3. Participative management supports decision making at the unit level, thereby fostering accountability
   4. Implementing participative management requires thorough staff education and frequent feedback on progress
   5. Nurses involved in this type of management model are responsible for implementing goals at the unit level; they should be committed to nursing as a career

X. Total Quality Management

A. General information
   1. Total Quality Management (TQM) is a philosophy of management developed by W. Edwards Deming
   2. Originally implemented in Japan after World War II, TQM is credited with the outstanding recovery of postwar Japanese industry
   3. TQM was introduced to various organizations in the United States in the 1970s
   4. Almost 70% of those organizations failed in their attempts to implement TQM

B. Key concepts
   1. Employees are given more authority over their work in a TQM system; individual employees have autonomy in decision making
   2. Employees are trained to make decisions that improve both the quality of the work and the productivity of the workers
   3. TQM embodies a paradigm shift from an emphasis on monitoring quality through scientific data collection to an ongoing, continuous measuring of quality through human responses to care
   4. Strategic planning for the future through the establishment of a long-term commitment to productivity and quality is the key to TQM
   5. TQM attempts to address the need for productivity and quality by meeting the concerns of both internal (employees) and external (clients) customers; organizational teamwork and individual empowerment are essential
   6. The focus of TQM is on results rather than on daily activities

---

FOURTEEN POINTS TO THE DEMING MANAGEMENT METHOD

1. Create and publish to all employees a statement of the aims and purposes of the company or other organization. The management must demonstrate constantly their commitment to this statement.
2. Learn the new philosophy, top management and everybody.
3. Understand the purpose of inspection, for improvement of processes and reduction of cost.
4. End the practice of awarding business on the basis of price tag alone.
5. Improve constantly and forever the system of production and service.
6. Institute training.
7. Teach and institute leadership.
8. Drive out fear. Create trust. Create a climate for innovation.

9. Optimize toward the aims and purposes of the company the efforts of teams, groups, staff areas.
10. Eliminate exhortations for the work force.
11 a. Eliminate numerical quotas for production. Instead, learn and institute methods for improvement.
11 b. Eliminate management by Objective. Instead, learn the capabilities of processes, and how to improve them.
12. Remove barriers that rob people of pride of workmanship.
13. Encourage edcuuation and self-improvement for everybody.
14. Take action to accompish the transformation.

Reprinted from *Out of the Crisis* by W. Edwards Deming by permission of MIT and The W. Edwards Deming Institute. Published by MIT, Center for Advanced Engineering Study, Cambridge, Mass. ©1986 by W. Edwards Deming.

C. Application to nursing
 1. The philosophy of TQM is summarized in Deming's "14 points" (see *Fourteen Points to the Deming Management Method*)
 2. Some hospitals are attempting to translate TQM into a model for management
 3. A shared governance structure within the nursing department best supports the management processes outlined by TQM
 4. TQM requires major system changes, including adoption of new organizational values
 5. It takes at least 5 years to adopt an organizational culture that promotes individual accountability and excellence
 6. The primary reason that so many industries, including health care organizations, fail to successfully implement TQM is management's reluctance to relinquish power and control

Points to remember

Management by objectives is both a management philosophy and a management method.

Decision-making models and trees provide effective approaches to problems.

Motivating employees is an important managerial skill.

Motivation derives from such factors as status, recognition, self-actualization, and affiliation.

According to the path-goal theory, the motivational function of management is to help employees see the relationship between personal and organizational goals, clarify the paths to accomplishing these goals, remove obstacles to goal achievement, and reward employees for work accomplished.

The directing and evaluating functions of management are shaped by managers' assumptions about their employees, assumptions that Douglas McGregor labeled Theory X and Theory Y.

The contingency model highlights the need for flexibility in leadership and management style.

Participative management decentralizes authority to the unit level.

Total Quality Management monitors quality through human responses to care.

Glossary

The following terms are defined in Appendix A, page 110.

decision rules	motivation
decision tree	Total Quality Management
legitimate power	

Study questions

To evaluate your understanding of this chapter, answer the following questions in the space provided; then compare your responses with the correct answers in Appendix B, pages 116 and 117.

1. According to the managerial grid, which management style is considered the most effective and why? _____

   _____

   _____

2. How are various management styles related to employee motivation? _____

   _____

   _____

3. Which model of management uses the concept of power in predicting the favorability of various situations for the manager? _____

   _____

   _____

4. Which type of overall organizational structure is crucial to a participate approach to management? _____

   _____

   _____

5. What factors are essential to successful implementation of a Total Quality Management approach? _____

   _____

   _____

CHAPTER 8

Processes in Leadership and Management

Learning objectives

Check off the following items once you've mastered them:

☐ Discuss the process of values clarification.

☐ Identify the characteristics of an assertive person.

☐ Describe the elements of performance appraisal and quality assurance.

☐ Identify the four components of an effective marketing plan.

☐ Define *networking*.

☐ Discuss the nurse manager's role in risk management.

☐ Identify the important components of team building, leading meetings, and interviewing.

I. Introduction

A. Processes used in leadership and management refer to those actions that enable a person to become a leader or manager or to improve skills

B. These processes incorporate important leadership and management concepts and methods

II. Values clarification

A. Key concepts
1. Using values clarification, a person examines, selects, and learns to act on principles and beliefs
2. Values clarification helps determine the importance or significance of an experience based on one's response to that experience
3. The values clarification process increases self-awareness and helps reaffirm a commitment to goals, increase self-confidence and autonomy, improve decision-making skills, and guide behavioral changes
4. Values clarification involves seven steps
   a. Step I: examining personal responses— emotional, intellectual, and physical—to experiences and interactions with others
   b. Step II: distinguishing between responses from internal (self) and external (others) sources
   c. Step III: reflecting on internal responses for consistency with personal values
   d. Step IV: accepting the need for change in attitude or behavior for consistency with personal values
   e. Step V: evaluating alternative ways to achieve these changes
   f. Step VI: developing behavior patterns consistent with internal responses and personal values
   g. Step VII: developing trust in personal feelings and intuition
B. Applications to nursing
1. Values clarification helps a nurse determine realistic goals—both personal and client-centered—to guide actions
2. A nurse leader or manager can use values clarification to identify group goals at the unit, departmental, and organizational levels
3. Values clarification enhances decision-making ability and enables expansion of skills, increasing expert power
4. Values clarification can help a nurse choose a work environment that reflects personal values

III. Assertiveness

A. Key concepts
1. Assertiveness is a process of communicating with self-confidence
2. It involves a balance between passiveness and aggressiveness

3. Assertiveness can be learned
4. An assertive person stands up for his or her rights but is careful not to infringe on the rights of others
5. An assertive person expresses feelings and needs clearly, honestly, and respectfully through I-MESSAGES, so that others have no doubts as to how their behavior affects the assertive person
6. An assertive person faces problems squarely and suggests solutions

B. Applications to nursing
1. A nurse leader or manager must be assertive to facilitate problem identification, problem solving, and decision making
2. A nurse leader or manager uses assertiveness to communicate staff needs to superiors
3. Assertive behavior by a nurse leader or manager often encourages staff to respond in the same fashion, promoting goal achievement
4. On a personal level, a nurse leader or manager can use assertiveness to manage stress, achieve a positive self-image, and improve professional productivity and job satisfaction

IV. Time management

A. Key concepts
1. Time management involves planning and scheduling for anticipated and unanticipated events in the workday
2. Effective time management hinges on priority setting and delegation
   a. Priority setting involves classifying activities and determining the optimal order in which they should be performed
   b. Delegation involves assigning duties and responsibilities to subordinates and making these subordinates accountable for their performance
3. Barriers to effective time management include interruptions and distractions, such as phone calls and visitors; learning to manage these interruptions is vital for effective time management

B. Applications to nursing
1. All nurses need to develop time management skills to work efficiently and provide optimal client care
2. Priorities for organizational goals are identified by a nurse manager's superiors and then delegated to the nurse manager for completion
3. Priorities for personal and unit goals are identified by a nurse manager
4. A nurse manager delegates duties and responsibilities to staff nurses, who in turn delegate duties and responsibilities to ancillary staff
5. A nurse manager who delegates to a staff nurse must give the staff nurse authority to perform the task
6. When a nurse manager delegates effectively, both the nurse manager and the subordinate are accountable for the result

7. Formal meetings and discussions should be set up by the nurse manager with a clear purpose, agenda, and time limit in mind, to minimize or prevent interruptions and distractions

V. Performance appraisal

A. Key concepts
   1. Performance appraisal is an integral part of management and provides an effective method of motivating employees and improving work performance
   2. It involves periodic evaluation of the strengths and weaknesses of a worker's job performance and is conducted by the worker's supervisor (who typically holds a line position in the organization)
   3. It involves objective and subjective factors
      a. *Objective* factors are measurable behaviors, such as lateness and absences
      b. *Subjective* factors are behaviors related to job performance, which the evaluator appraises and rates, usually using a checklist or rating scale; emphasis should be on observable behaviors and not on personality factors

B. Applications to nursing
   1. Nurse managers need in-depth training in performance appraisal to avoid bias and prejudice
   2. Assessment of a staff nurse's performance should be ongoing
   3. Corrective action, if necessary, should focus on helping the staff nurse set goals for improved performance
   4. The nurse manager can select the best example of a nurse's performance and apply that example as a standard to improve performance; this is known as *benchmarking*

VI. Quality assurance

A. Key concepts
   1. In health care, quality assurance is an evaluation of client care
   2. Quality assurance includes self-evaluation, performance appraisal, peer review, audits, and utilization review; it operationalizes accountability at the individual, unit, and organizational levels
   3. The need for quality assurance in health care has intensified with rising costs
   4. In hospitals, quality assurance programs are based on outcome and process standards established by the American Nurses Association (ANA), the American Hospital Association, and the Joint Commission on Accreditation of Health Care Organizations (JCAHO)
   5. Quality assurance initially focused on the cost and quality of care received by clients in the Medicare, Medicaid, and maternal-child health programs

6. Quality assurance programs focus on *structure*, the setting in which client care is delivered; *process*, the manner in which care is delivered; and *outcome*, the results of that care
7. Quality assurance involves setting STANDARDS, establishing criteria, and evaluating performance
   a. Setting standards involves the ANA Standards of Nursing Practice and specific standards or objectives for the client population
   b. Establishing criteria involves determining how the standards are to be met
   c. Evaluating performance involves either concurrent audits to evaluate ongoing care or retrospective audits to evaluate care after clients are discharged
8. JCAHO mandates retrospective audits of discharged clients' charts to determine if various outcome criteria were met
9. Every quality assurance program should have a mechanism for corrective action that addresses unmet outcome criteria

B. Applications to nursing
1. Nurse managers and leaders play an active role in quality assurance through peer reviews and performance appraisals
2. A nurse manager should explain to the staff in advance what outcome criteria will be used in evaluation
3. A nurse manager should work with the staff to implement corrective action for unmet criteria

VII. Continuous Quality Improvement

A. Key concepts
1. The Total Quality Management approach involves transforming old quality assurance programs into newer systems that reflect a continuous striving for quality
2. Quality assurance is being replaced by such terms as *total quality improvement, continuous quality improvement,* and *quality assessment improvement*
3. These new programs emphasize teamwork over individual performance
4. In a Continuous Quality Improvement (CQI) approach, accountability flows upward from the point of service to administration
   a. CQI encompasses both centralized and decentralized activities that cut across all disciplines involved in client care
   b. In a CQI program, data are collected and analyzed to address the functioning of an entire system rather than focusing on the individual performance criteria of quality assurance; the functional criteria of CQI, in turn, emphasizes care that is appropriate, effective, and adequate to meet client care
   c. In CQI, benchmarking is used to select a standard of excellence for a process or procedure; that standard is used to measure related processes or procedures

   5. Whereas the focus of care under quality assurance is on controlling
       quality, the focus of care under CQI is on measuring the
       appropriateness of care
       a. Both quality control and appropriateness measures are essential
       b. Similar to quality assurance, CQI emphasizes both process and
           outcome standards
   B. Applications to nursing
       1. Staff nurses play a fundamental role in a CQI system; the nurse
           identifies problems, collects data, establishes plans to ensure
           performance and client outcomes, and evaluates the plan of care
       2. Nurses have an ongoing obligation to establish uniform standards of
           quality in client care outcomes

VIII. Marketing

   A. Key concepts
       1. Marketing includes analysis, planning, implementation, and control of a
           specialized program designed to provide an exchange of goods, services,
           or values within a specific arena while achieving organizational goals
       2. Exchange of goods requires at least two parties, each believing that
           the other has something of value and each being capable of
           communication, delivery, and acceptance or rejection of the offer
       3. The communication describes the services provided and targets these
           services to specific population needs
       4. Marketing is achieved through a MARKETING PLAN
           a. A successful marketing plan involves the "four Ps": product, price,
               place, and promotion
           b. Periodic evaluation of the marketing plan allows the organization to
               meet the changing needs of the target population
   B. Applications to nursing
       1. Because cost containment and competition have caused health care
           organizations to promote their services to the public, nursing has
           become an integral part of each organization's marketing plan
       2. Nurses, especially nurse managers, are required to sell themselves as
           providers of health care to consumers and to the health care organization
       3. As health care consumers become more aware of health care options
           and more selective, nurses at all levels must promote themselves
           effectively so that the public knows just what they do
       4. Nurse managers play a vital role in nursing recruitment and retention
           and thus can enhance a health care organization's marketability as a
           provider of quality care
       5. A nurse manager also may be responsible for the development and
           promotion of additional programs to broaden the scope of a health
           care organization's services, thereby contributing to its profitability

IX. Networking

A. Key concepts
1. Networking refers to the development and use of a professional system for support, guidance, and information to help achieve growth
2. Successful networking requires a positive self-concept, self-awareness, and values clarification
3. A network can include individuals and groups
4. Networking involves role-modeling, power, and politics
5. A person who networks effectively combines the innate tendency to help others with a willingness to use others and, in turn, be used by others in the network

B. Applications to nursing
1. Nurse managers often are members of a staff nurse's network
2. Nurse managers in turn have their own network from which to derive support at the unit, department, organizational, and professional levels
3. Nurse managers and leaders use the concepts of power and politics in networking

X. Mentoring

A. Key concepts
1. Just as networking provides a mechanism for professional support, mentoring provides a mechanism for professional growth
2. Mentoring is a relationship between an experienced nurse (the mentor) and a novice nurse (the protégé); the mentor guides and prepares the protégé for personal and professional advancement
3. Mentoring provides various support mechanisms, including advice, friendship, counseling, and contacts; it paves the way for developing self-confidence and commitment to personal and professional self-actualization, the highest form of motivation
4. Mentoring is different from preceptoring in that preceptoring is a form of staff orientation whereby new nurses learn the tasks and the system from experienced nurses

B. Applications to nursing
1. Mentoring has not been a common phenomenon in nursing
2. Nurses, and women in general, have suffered from a lack of mentors in all areas of professional life, which may contribute to a diminished sense of job satisfaction

XI. Risk management

A. Key concepts
1. Risk management is a business strategy to reduce or prevent loss and legal action by identifying, analyzing, and evaluating risks and developing plans for reducing the frequency and severity of accidents and injury

2. Health care organizations use risk management to ensure quality control in care delivery and to prevent liability by providing a safe environment and adequate, competent staff members
3. The purpose of risk management in health care is to identify the variables that jeopardize quality care and to correct or minimize them
4. Risk management involves communication, decision making, and change
5. Accountability is the central issue in risk management
6. Successful risk management requires effective communication among all levels of an organization
7. Components of risk management include monitoring devices such as audits, grievances, staffing patterns, and employee and client INCIDENT REPORTS

B. Applications to nursing
1. A nurse manager is legally responsible for observing, evaluating, and reporting deficiencies in client care
2. Reporting threats to client or employee safety is a major responsibility of nurses at all levels; such threats should be documented in the client's chart and in incident reports
3. A nurse must file an incident report whenever safety or quality is jeopardized; client injury, staff injury, or medication error must be documented
4. A nurse manager should investigate all incident reports and be alert to deficient care
5. A nurse manager should assure staff nurses that incident reports are used to avoid litigation and ensure quality care, not as a means to discipline or evaluate staff members
6. Educating staff nurses in proper documentation is the nurse manager's responsibility

XII. Stress management

A. Key concepts
1. Stress management involves coping with the body's response to conflict (stress)
2. Stress can be of several sorts: task-based stress, such as work overload; role-based stress, such as conflict between professional and personal roles; institution-based stress, such as understaffing; and personal stress, such as conflict between expectations of performance and perception of that performance
3. Stress is impossible to avoid and is not necessarily harmful
4. Stress can be a positive force (eustress) that adds excitement and challenge to life or a negative force (distress) that impairs effectiveness
5. Accumulation of high stress levels without appropriate management can lead to BURNOUT

B. Applications to nursing

1. A nurse manager should work at the unit, departmental, and organizational levels to minimize or eliminate potential stressors
2. A nurse manager can use a knowledge of conflict resolution, decision making, and networking to develop stress management strategies
3. A nurse manager should teach staff members how to identify sources of stress and eliminate or minimize these stressors
4. A nurse manager should act as a role model to help staff nurses manage stress
5. A nurse manager can help prevent personal distress and burnout by establishing realistic personal and professional goals and priorities

XIII. Team building

A. Key concepts
  1. Team building develops a supportive group atmosphere in which members work together effectively toward specific goals
  2. Planning, setting goals, and establishing priorities are the first steps in team building
  3. GROUP COHESIVENESS is the foundation of team building
  4. Communication and group dynamics are essential to team building, group cohesiveness, and team effectiveness
  5. The greater the cohesiveness among team members, the greater the group's influence on goal achievement and the greater the group's job satisfaction among individual members
  6. Team members are selected for their ability to contribute to the team

B. Applications to nursing
  1. A nurse leader or manager should use knowledge of group communication and dynamics to develop a climate that fosters group cohesiveness
  2. A nurse leader or manager should assist the team with conflict management and resolution within the team and with other teams
  3. A nurse leader or manager should encourage open communication within the team and with other teams

XIV. Leading meetings

A. Key concepts
  1. Meetings may be called to discuss and solve problems, ventilate feelings, educate, or share information
  2. Planning and organization are essential; an effective meeting should have a set agenda with specific objectives, and it should begin and end on time, allowing for summary and evaluation
  3. Leading meetings requires knowledge of power, authority, influence, group dynamics, communication, decision making, and leadership and management styles
  4. The person leading the meeting has authority and power and should use a leadership style that enhances the meeting's effectiveness

5. The leader should act as both a leader and a group member in working to achieve the meeting's objectives
6. The environment of the meeting room should be comfortable and allow for group interaction and communication

B. Applications to nursing
1. A nurse leader or manager should participate in meetings to train staff, resolve conflicts, provide motivation, and encourage discussion—which may mean mixing roles as a leader and a group member
2. An effective nurse leader or manager uses a knowledge of leadership and management styles, communication, and group dynamics to achieve meeting objectives
3. A nurse leader or manager uses power to assist group functioning
4. A nurse leader or manager should communicate the outcome of the meeting to the appropriate personnel and take the necessary steps to implement the outcome at the appropriate level

XV. Interviewing

A. Key concepts
1. Interviewing is a step in selecting persons for positions in an organization
2. Evaluation of information obtained from interviews forms the basis for hiring decisions
3. Interviewing involves dual communication; the interviewer seeks to gain and evaluate information from the applicant, and the applicant attempts to gather information about the position and the organization
4. An effective interviewer can solicit information efficiently and gather relevant data
5. A successful interview requires up-front planning and organization, clear communication about the position and the organization and its goals, and an interest and trust in the applicant

B. Applications to nursing
1. Nurse managers typically play a significant role in staff recruitment and hiring decisions
2. The organizational structure directly affects the nurse manager's power and authority to interview and hire
3. Conversely, nurse managers often can influence organizational hiring policies
4. A nurse manager communicates information about the health care organization's structure and goals to applicants

Points to remember

Values clarification and assertiveness result in self-awareness and self-confidence.

Effective time management is essential to effective managing.

Performance appraisals and quality assurance are important parts of a manager's evaluation function.

The emphasis on cost containment in health care delivery has increased the need to market nursing services.

Effectiveness in team building and leading meetings is based on mastering group dynamics.

Glossary

The following terms are defined in Appendix A, page 110.

burnout	incident report
group cohesiveness	marketing plan
I-messages	standard

Study questions

To evaluate your understanding of this chapter, answer the following questions in the space provided; then compare your responses with the correct answers in Appendix B, page 117.

1. How are values clarification and assertiveness related to time management?

   _____

   _____

2. What is benchmarking and how is it applied in both performance appraisal and Continuous Quality Improvement? _____

   _____

   _____

3. What two standards are emphasized by both Quality Assurance and Continuous Quality Improvement programs? _____

   _____

4. How does a mentor relationship enhance individual motivation? _____

   _____

   _____

CHAPTER 9

Budgeting and Resource Allocation

Learning objectives

Check off the following items once you've mastered them:

☐ Define *budget*.

☐ Describe the common approaches to budgeting.

☐ Identify the major types of budgets.

☐ Describe the nurse manager's role in budgeting.

I. Introduction

A. Budgeting involves planning and controlling resources that affect the workings of an organization

B. Budgeting is accomplished through a plan called a BUDGET

C. A budget is a detailed outline that describes planned organizational goals and compares them with actual outcomes
   1. It attempts to identify problems and determine steps to correct them
   2. It provides communication among all levels of managers and their subordinates
   3. It shows how resources will be acquired and used over specific intervals
   4. It ensures the availability of necessary resources for goal achievement
   5. It promotes smooth and efficient organizational operation for goal achievement
   6. It acts as a tool for management to make modifications and changes and to project activities necessary for coordinating and achieving organizational goals
   7. It helps management control the organization by allocating resources

D. A budget translates organizational goals and outcomes into monetary values to ensure that monies spent (EXPENDITURES) do not exceed monies received (*income*) within a given period
   1. In a budget, money is divided into two categories: income and expenditures
   2. Income and expenditures are further divided into subcategories
   3. These subcategories may differ according to the service provided by the organization and the approach used for budgeting
   4. The desired outcome of any budget is to optimize resources and minimize variance; the optimal use of resources is determined by the accuracy of the initial BUDGET FORECAST and the ongoing evaluation and revision of the budget.

E. Two commonly used approaches to budgeting are INCREMENTAL BUDGETING and *zero-based budgeting*
   1. Incremental budgeting
      a. In this traditional budgeting process, a budget is developed annually based on the expenditures from the previous year
      b. Income and expenditures from the previous year are analyzed and reasons for deviations from the previous budget allocations are evaluated
      c. Projections are made based on the organization's plans and goals, such as salary increases and expansion; these projections usually increase monetary allocations
      d. Dollar figures for income and expenditures are assigned to these projections

e. The completed budget must be approved by the head of the organization

f. Anyone with the authority to spend money is required to work within the budget; adjustments may be made but typically are resisted

2. Zero-based budgeting
   a. This is a participative process based on the assumption that every expenditure must be justified as essential to the organization's function each year; expenditures for the previous year are irrelevant
   b. Each year, the budget begins at zero
   c. Tools called DECISION PACKAGES are compiled and assigned priorities based on the organizational goals and available resources and then implemented
   d. Zero-based budgeting requires more precise planning and allows for more participation than incremental budgeting; it also requires more work and time to complete than incremental budgeting

II. Capital expenditure budgets

A. Key concepts
   1. Capital expenditure budgets allocate monies to purchase major equipment or finance major projects such as expansion or renovation; these monies are called *capital expenditures*
   2. Capital expenditure items usually are major investments that entail long-term cost recovery
   3. Capital expenditure budgets typically involve two common criteria: the proposed item must be above a certain specified cost and must have a specified life expectancy, usually several years
   4. Capital expenditure budgets require long-range planning

B. Applications to nursing
   1. A nurse manager can help anticipate and determine the need for capital expenditures in a health care organization by maintaining close communication with other departments and by keeping current with technological advances and trends
   2. A nurse manager must know the budgetary limits on capital expenditures when establishing priorities
   3. A nurse manager completes capital expenditure request forms, using information such as depreciation, salvage value, and age of equipment to justify requests

III. Operating budgets

A. Key concepts
   1. Operating budgets allocate monies required to support organizational operation; the two principal operating expenditures are personnel and supplies and equipment
   2. An organization's operating budget deals primarily with salaries, supplies, and contractual services
   3. Other items, such as time, materials, work hours, and personnel, can be translated into dollar values as part of the operating budget

B. Applications to nursing
   1. Nurse managers play an important role in determining operating budgets
   2. With today's emphasis on cost containment in health care, nurse managers are assuming more responsibility for developing operating budgets and controlling operating costs
   3. Because of their direct involvement with staffing and scheduling, nurse managers can anticipate needs and justify requests for staffing increases
   4. The nurse manager works with staff members to identify changing supply requirements and communicates these changes to superiors
   5. The nurse manager monitors the use of equipment and supplies and recommends to the staff ways to minimize costs at the unit level
   6. The nurse manager should be aware that health care organizations are hiring hospital managemenet companies to help manage the budgetary pressures of contending with rising costs and reimbursement systems
      a. These companies develop strategic plans of 2 to 5 years' duration to ensure cost control, quality control, and competitiveness
      b. These strategic plans are translated into an operating budget that has as a goal the accurate forecasting of fiscal needs, with an emphasis on external events that affect these fiscal needs

Points to remember

Budgeting involves the managerial functions of planning and controlling.

Two common approaches to budgeting are incremental budgeting and zero-based budgeting.

Capital expenditures can include major equipment, expansion, and renovations.

Operating budgets include items such as salaries, supplies, personnel, work hours, materials, and time.

Nurse managers play a significant role in influencing budgets.

Glossary

The following terms are defined in Appendix A, page 110.

budget

budget forecast

decision package

expenditures

incremental budgeting

Study questions

To evaluate your understanding of this chapter, answer the following questions in the space provided; then compare your responses with the correct answers in Appendix B, page 117.

1. What is the desired outcome of any organizational budget? _____

_____

_____

2. How does zero-based budgeting differ from incremental budgeting?

_____

_____

3. What are the two principal expenditures in an operating budget?

_____

_____

CHAPTER 10

Staffing and Scheduling

Learning objectives

Check off the following items once you've mastered them:

☐ Define *staffing*.

☐ Identify the two major types of staffing.

☐ Explain variable and cyclical work schedules.

☐ Discuss the nurse manager's role in each type of staffing.

I. Introduction

A. Staffing refers to the number and mix of nursing personnel required for a nursing unit to provide safe, quality, 24-hour client care

B. Staffing is determined by
1. Number and mix of personnel available
2. CLIENT CENSUS
3. Type of client care delivery system in use
4. Levels of CLIENT ACUITY

C. Levels of client acuity are critical to determining the number and type of staff needed to ensure quality care
1. Various patient classification systems (PCSs) are used to provide data on the level, complexity, and actual costs of care
2. Some of the PCSs in use include GRASP, Medicus, and APACHE
3. PCSs can be used to justify the number and qualifications of needed staff
   a. If PCSs are properly managed, nurse managers can objectively quantify nursing in terms of "costing out services"
   b. Costing out services is essential for justifying the need for skilled nursing care and obtaining reimbursement for that care

D. Adequate staffing is essential for quality client care — the ultimate goal of any health care organization

E. Securing adequate staffing involves developing a work schedule; an effective work schedule enhances nurses' job satisfaction

F. A work schedule can be *cyclical* or *variable*
1. A CYCLICAL WORK SCHEDULE repeats basic elements over a specified period
   a. Personnel are scheduled to work a specific number of days with specific days off
   b. A cyclical schedule enables personnel to know their schedules in advance and plan accordingly
   c. Cyclical schedules usually are made months in advance
2. A VARIABLE WORK SCHEDULE changes continually, based on changing staffing needs
   a. Personnel are scheduled according to client census, client acuity levels, and level of nursing skill required
   b. Variable schedules use nursing pools, part-time help, and "floats" to supplement the regular staff

G. Staffing structure may be *centralized* or *decentralized*, depending on the organizational structure

II. Centralized staffing

A. General information
1. Centralized staffing allocates personnel by a SCHEDULER, often using a computer
2. Centralized staffing applies to all nursing units within an organization
3. It involves consistent, objective, and fair application of organizational policies to all personnel
4. It provides opportunities for cost containment through better use of resources

B. Advantages of centralized staffing
1. Treats employees fairly and impartially by maintaining consistent staffing policies
2. Enables preparation of schedules that effectively meet organizational goals
3. Aids cost containment and time management
4. Relieves managers from many time-consuming duties
5. Promotes less frequent special requests from staff for changes in work schedules

C. Disadvantages of centralized staffing
1. May create or bring out other organizational or managerial problems
2. Does not address individual workers' abilities, knowledge level, and interests
3. Does not address variable nursing care needs in particular units

D. Applications to nursing
1. In a centralized staffing system, the nurse manager typically is responsible for developing a master staffing pattern, clarifying job descriptions, managing personnel, and controlling the personnel budget
2. The nurse manager must communicate these needs and any changes to the scheduler to ensure adequate staffing

III. Decentralized staffing

A. General information
1. Decentralized staffing allocates personnel at the unit level rather than at the organizational level
2. Decentralized staffing is congruent with continuous quality improvement; accountability flows from the point of service upward to the administrative levels
3. With decentralized staffing, a unit manager has the authority and the responsibility to secure adequate personnel for the unit

    4. Decentralized staffing is based on sharing and requires efficient time management; resources may be used less efficiently if time management is inefficient

B. Advantages of decentralized staffing
    1. Enables preparation of individualized schedules based on knowledge of the unit and personnel
    2. Makes the head nurse or nurse manager accountable for staffing decisions
    3. Enables greater control of activities and rapid schedule adjustments based on changing needs

C. Disadvantages of decentralized staffing
    1. May be more time consuming for the nurse manager than centralized staffing
    2. May result in insufficient staffing to meet unforeseen needs
    3. May invite excessive special requests by staff for individualized schedules, making scheduling difficult and time consuming

D. Applications to nursing
    1. In a decentralized staffing system, the nurse manager is directly responsible for establishing the personnel allotments and schedules
    2. In decentralized staffing, a nurse manager must be aware of his or her role both as the manager and as a group member
    3. Especially in a decentralized staffing system, the nurse manager evaluates the effectiveness of unit staffing and recommends needed changes
    4. Decentralized staffing requires a nurse manager to have excellent time management and communication skills

Points to remember

Adequate staffing and effective scheduling are essential to providing quality client care.

Staffing may be centralized or decentralized, depending on the organizational structure.

Work schedules may be cyclical or variable.

The nurse manager plays a major role in centralized or decentralized staffing.

Glossary

The following terms are defined in Appendix A, page 110.

tclient acuity

client census

cyclical work schedule

scheduler

variable work schedule

Study questions

To evaluate your understanding of this chapter, answer the following questions in the space provided; then compare your responses with the correct answers in Appendix B, pages 117 and 118.

1. On what is staffing determined? _____

_____

_____

2. How do patient classification systems (PCSs) help in the professionalization of nursing? _____

_____

3. How does decentralized staffing relate to Continuous Quality Improvement?

_____

_____

CHAPTER 11

The Changing Health Care Delivery System

Learning objectives

Check off the following items once you've mastered them:

☐ Discuss how economic change is affecting health care organizations and nursing practice.

☐ Identify the significant demographic changes that are affecting health care delivery and nursing practice.

☐ Identify the changes resulting from the increasing use of advanced technology in health care, and discuss how these changes are affecting nursing practice.

I. Introduction

A. The last decade has been characterized by widespread changes in all aspects of health care that have restructured the health care delivery system and dramatically affected nursing practice

B. The most significant changes—in economics, demographics, and technology—have fragmented health care services

C. Establishing an organized, comprehensive approach to health care delivery is the mandate for the future

D. Nurse leaders and managers can play an essential role in developing this new approach to health care delivery

II. Economic change

A. Key concepts
1. During the last decade, total health care expenditures in the United States have more than doubled
2. This increase has resulted not from improved health care but from inefficient use of resources
3. Federally mandated efforts to reduce expenditures under Medicare legislation have created PROSPECTIVE PAYMENT SYSTEMS (PPSs) and DIAGNOSIS-RELATED GROUPS (DRGs)
4. Increasing consumer demand for quality services despite cost containment has increased competition among health care organizations
5. Private insurers and large corporations also are demanding cost containment and cost-effectiveness
6. Consumers are increasingly demanding excellence and accountability from all health care providers

B. Applications to nursing
1. Emphasizing cost containment, health care organizations are operating like businesses; consequently, nurses must understand business management concepts and processes
2. Because nursing services account for nearly half the expenditures of health care organizations, nursing departments are pressured to reduce costs while increasing productivity
3. Nurse leaders and managers must become skilled at predicting budgetary and staffing needs in order to use resources efficiently
4. Nurse leaders and managers must represent their subordinates on committees that determine financial and resource allocation
5. Nurse leaders and managers must stress the need for sufficient nursing staff to ensure quality client care
6. The economic changes affecting health care challenge nurse leaders and managers to better define nursing practice and to obtain reimbursement for nursing services

7. Nurse leaders and managers are challenged to document and publicize the cost-effectiveness of various types of nursing care, such as care provided by nurse practitioners, nurse midwives, and nurse anesthetists

III. Demographic change

A. Key concepts
1. Changes in the demographic composition of the American population have spurred changes in social, economic, and health care policies and practices
2. The rapidly increasing older population places new burdens on the health care delivery system, such as a demand for home care services and senior day-care centers
3. The significant increase in single-parent families, especially households headed by women, creates new issues for society and the delivery of health care, resulting in increased demand for services such as day care and for more flexible policies such as parental leave for childbirth
4. An increasing minority population expands the need for health care services
5. Certain demographic trends suggest widening poverty in the United States, decreasing the availability of and accessibility to health care services to those who may have great need for such services

B. Applications to nursing
1. The effect of various demographic changes will alter the scope of nursing practice, shifting nursing practice from hospital-based to community-based care and creating more independent and diversified roles that require strong leadership and managerial skills
2. Nursing's holistic approach to health care provides an excellent foundation for addressing the health needs of a changing population
3. Demographic changes will necessitate expanding alternative health care services, creating new opportunities for nursing to expand its role in the health care delivery system
4. Client needs will direct nursing services toward a HEALTH PROMOTION–disease prevention model of care
5. Nursing practice increasingly will focus on health education and self-care models, which should expand nurses' roles, responsibilities, and power
6. Nurses must become more active in planning and making policy decisions affecting health care
7. In the area of ethics, nurses must be aware that the need for expanded services and the reality of limited resources will force nurses to participate in decisions about who may and may not receive health care services

IV. Technological change

A. Key concepts
   1. The rapid proliferation of computer information systems is increasing the knowledge base at a phenomenal rate
   2. The increasing use of computers in health care organizations is changing the roles of all health care practitioners and improving the efficiency and cost-effectiveness of certain services
   3. Computers can provide up-to-the-minute information about client census, acuity levels, budgetary issues, availability of resources and equipment, and staffing needs; this enables more rapid and more informed decision making at all organizational levels
   4. The ever-increasing sophistication and complexity of equipment used in disease diagnosis, treatment, and client care require ongoing education for all health care practitioners
   5. Advanced technology in health care also requires new protocols and procedures for effective management of client care

B. Applications to nursing
   1. The increasing use of computers in health care organizations mandates that all nurses be computer literate
   2. Nurse managers find computers invaluable tools for planning, organizing, directing, and evaluating
   3. Computers can efficiently perform routine, time-consuming tasks, freeing nurses for more creative and productive activities
   4. Computerized information systems provide nurse managers with a constant flow of current information and access to instant communication, which can help speed organizational change
   5. Technological advances have created new and highly specialized nursing roles, which in turn are changing the lines of communication and decision-making authority within health care organizations
   6. Newly specialized nursing roles require ongoing education and retraining for nurses
   7. Increasingly sophisticated and complex health care technology often requires nurses to coordinate client care among numerous health care disciplines

V. Proposed health care reform

A. Key concepts
   1. A national health reform proposal, the American Health Security Act of 1993, has been introduced into Congress
   2. This act is the federal government's attempt to control rising health care costs and provide adequate health care coverage for all citizens
   3. On a national level, providers and payors are to form partnerships as managed care units that will offer both health care and health insurance as a single product

4. A National Health Board will be established to register these partnerships and oversee provision of uniform health care benefits
5. On a state level, employers will be required to provide insurance coverage to full-time employees; small businesses will be required to join state-approved health insurance purchasing cooperatives
6. If enacted, many modifications of the existing act are anticipated
7. Regardless of the outcome or form that the health care reform proposal takes, managed care and managed competition are a reality in health care today

B. Applications to nursing
1. Until recently, the prevailing payment method for health care services was fee for service, with insurance companies paying for client care
2. With managed care, insurance companies, HEALTH MAINTENANCE ORGANIZATIONS (HMOs), and employers have several payment options, including CAPITATION, PER DIEM, and CASE RATES
   a. With each of these payment options, the health care organization must compete for clients by identifying quality indicators and implementing cost controls
   b. With each of these payment options, the health care organization is liable for the cost of excessive treatment
3. Nurses will have to work closely with Quality Assurance and Utilization Review committees, while adhering faithfully to the Joint Commission on Accreditation of Health Care Organizations guidelines
4. Documentation of nursing care, particularly the documentation of outcome and cost, becomes even more vital in a managed care setting

Points to remember

Significant changes in economics, demographics, and technology are profoundly affecting health care delivery and nursing practice.

Economic changes primarily involve cost containment and cost effectiveness.

Various demographic changes, such as the increasing number of older and minority populations and single-family households, will alter the scope of nursing practice.

Technological changes—specifically, the use of computers and advanced equipment in health care delivery—are altering nurses' decision-making responsibilities and communication lines.

Glossary

The following terms are defined in Appendix A, page 110.

capitation rate	health promotion
case rate	per diem rate
diagnosis-related group (DRG)	prospective payment system (PPS)
health maintenance organization (HMO)	

Study questions

To evaluate your understanding of this chapter, answer the following questions in the space provided; then compare your responses with the correct answers in Appendix B, page 118.

1. How have economic changes affected the health care delivery system?

_____

_____

2. How have demographic changes affected the scope of nursing practice?

_____

_____

3. What is the American Health Security Act of 1993? _____

_____

_____

CHAPTER 12

Issues in Nursing Leadership and Management

Learning objectives

Check off the following items once you've mastered them:

☐ Describe the collective bargaining process.

☐ Describe the steps involved in a grievance procedure.

☐ Define the role a budget plays in cost containment.

☐ Define *staffing*.

I. Introduction

A. Consumers, government, and third-party payors demand quality health care in a safe environment

B. In today's atmosphere of cost containment, quality care must also be cost-effective care

C. Nurses are becoming increasingly accountable for ensuring quality care

D. Health care organizations are accountable for providing an environment that promotes quality care

E. The quality of care can be monitored through a quality control program

F. Employee grievances, collective bargaining, cost containment, and staffing are important components of a quality control program

G. Quality control of nursing care at the unit level is primarily the nurse manager's responsibility

H. Health care organizations that do not meet employee demands for an effective and safe work environment may become the target of COLLECTIVE BARGAINING efforts to improve working conditions

II. Collective bargaining

A. Key concepts
   1. Collective bargaining provides a means for workers and management to meet and solve conflicts about working conditions, wages, work load, hours, and various GRIEVANCES
   2. Collective bargaining is a legal process carried out through a union or other labor organization
   3. Collective bargaining results in a labor agreement or contract that specifies the rights and responsibilities of both workers and management
   4. An increasing number of health care institutions are participating in collective bargaining
   5. The National Labor Relations Act of 1935 (also known as the Wagner Act) established the right of workers to join unions and created the National Labor Relations Board (NLRB), whose purpose is to enforce the act and curb unfair labor practices
      a. In 1967, the NLRB was given jurisdiction over proprietary hospitals and nursing homes; in 1975, the NLRB was given jurisdiction over nonprofit hospitals
      b. The NLRB resolves disputes between an employer and a bargaining unit; if an agreement is not reached but both parties are unwilling to compromise, the bargaining unit may decide to strike in hopes of forcing the employer to make concessions

6. The American Nurses Association (ANA) established an Economic Security Program in 1946, which established national salary guidelines for nurses
7. Health care workers have become increasingly involved in unions, and nurses have begun to organize and strike through state nurses' groups
8. In most instances, health care workers form or join unions to help gain fair pay, job security, and good working conditions
9. Nurses tend to form or join unions for economic and professional reasons, typically related to frustration concerning a perceived lack of control over their practice and lack of input into decision making in health care organizations
10. In health care organizations, a notice to strike must be given 10 days before the strike; a request for any change in the collective bargaining agreement requires 90 days' written notice (compared with the 60 days' notice required in other industries)

B. Applications to nursing
1. Nurses should be aware of and clarify their own values regarding collective bargaining and strikes when choosing a workplace
2. Nurses also need to protect themselves from unfair management practices
3. Nurses working in a health care organization with a collective bargaining agreement should obtain and study a copy of the collective bargaining contract, which specifies conditions of employment, such as salaries, work load, fringe benefits, and advancement opportunities, as well as specific procedures for filing grievances regarding various issues
4. Collective bargaining contracts establish *nurse practice committees,* which allow employees to become involved in health care decisions
5. A nurse manager should review past positions taken by both the union and management on contract negotiations, grievances, and decisions to strike; this information can help the nurse manager identify and address key issues before they become problematic
6. In a health care organization that displays minimal concern for employee satisfaction, a nurse leader may become instrumental in lobbying for a collective bargaining agreement

III. Employee grievances

A. Key concepts
1. A labor agreement or contract typically specifies a detailed procedure for filing employee grievances
2. Grievances generally fall into two categories: unfair labor practices or violations of a contract, precedent, or past practice
3. A grievance may represent a violation of the contract or a misunderstanding of the contract, or it may be a means of expressing employee dissatisfaction
4. The grievance procedure typically begins with an informal discussion between the employee and the manager

5. If informal communication fails to resolve the issue, the next step is formal communication (a written appeal), followed by a meeting of the employee, a management representative, and a union representative
6. If the grievance remains unresolved, it goes to a neutral third party for ARBITRATION

B. Applications to nursing
1. Nurses who participate in a grievance procedure need to learn and use the concepts of conflict resolution, communication, decision making, and group dynamics
2. When initiating a grievance procedure, the nurse should know and use the formal channels of oral and written communication
3. A thorough analysis of the grievance along with an exploration of similar instances in the past should guide the nurse manager in decision making
4. Resolution of a grievance should result in a *win-win solution* for the nurse and nursing management; this will create a constructive climate for future grievance procedures
5. A contract provides a solution to employee grievances; the nurse manager must base decisions on contract stipulations, rather than on personal power or authority (see *Legitimate Grievances*, page 106)

IV. Cost containment

A. Key concepts
1. The economic changes in health care over the last decade have created a climate of competition for funding and resources among health care organizations
2. Cost containment involves minimizing expenditures and maximizing efficiency; at the unit level, nurses are pressured to curtail cost while increasing efficiency
3. Because nursing care is not a separate reimbursable item but is instead included in the client's room rate, cost containment of nursing at the unit level is difficult
4. Identifying clear, measurable nursing goals—such as those in a management-by-objectives (MBO) system—along with various cost accounting measures may help contain nursing expenditures
   a. MBO focuses on maximizing the efficiency and quality of care
   b. Cost accounting focuses on critically analyzing expenses with an eye toward improving the use of resources
5. Gainsharing—giving employees a financial incentive by allowing them to share in the institution's profits—is one way of making employees more conscious of measures to improve efficiency and reduce waste
6. Cost containment requires managerial planning and evaluation through a budget, which serves as a plan for using resources and an evaluation of how the resources have been used

LEGITIMATE GRIEVANCES

Below are examples of five categories of legitimate employee grievances.

Contract violations

Your employment contract is binding on you *and* your employer. If your employer violates the contract, you have a valid grievance. In the following examples, assume that the contract prohibits the employer action described:
• You're performing the charge nurse's job 2 or 3 days a week but still receiving the same pay as other staff nurses.
• You've had to work undesirable shifts or on Sundays more often than other nurses.
• Your supervisor doesn't post time schedules in advance.
• Your employer discharges you without just cause.

Federal and state law violations

Any action by your employer that violates a federal or state law would be the basis for a grievance, even if your contract permits the action. For example:
• A female nurse receives less pay for performing the same work as a male nurse.
• You don't receive overtime pay that you're entitled to.
• Your employer doesn't promote you because of your race.

Past practice violations

A past practice—one that's been accepted by both parties over an extended period and is suddenly discontinued by the employer without notification—may be the basis for a grievance. For example:
• Your employer charges you for breaking equipment when others haven't been charged.
• Your employer revokes parking lot privileges.
• Your employer eliminates a rotation system for float assignments.
   A past practice violation can occur even if the past practice isn't specified in the contract. If the practice violates the contract, either party can demand that the contract be enforced. If the practice is unsafe, an arbitrator may simply abolish it.

Health and safety violations

Grievances in this category most often involve working conditions that an employer is responsible for, even if the contract doesn't cover the specific complaint. For example:
• You're required to hold clients during X-rays.
• You have no hand-washing facilities near client rooms.

Employer policy violations

Your employer can't violate its own rules without being guilty of a grievance, even though it can change the rules unilaterally. For example:
• You haven't received a performance evaluation in 2 years, although your employee handbook states that such evaluations will be done annually.
• Your employer assigns you a vacation period without your consent, contrary to personnel policies.

B. Applications to nursing
   1. Nurse leaders and managers should understand their health care organization's formal structure, philosophy, and objectives, all of which influence the operating budget

2. The budget outlines a way for a nurse manager to achieve individual and organizational goals; meeting these goals promotes job satisfaction

3. Resource use is enhanced by a knowledge of economic, demographic, and technological changes in health care, which helps the nurse manager predict operating costs

4. Involving staff nurses in cost containment by sharing budget information and budgetary goals is a wise nursing management strategy

5. Encouraging staff participation in cost containment helps motivate staff nurses to work more efficiently and productively, especially when the budget allows for staff education, research, and innovation in care

V. Inadequate staffing

A. Key concepts
   1. Staffing involves determining the number and mix of nurses needed on a unit to provide quality client care 24 hours a day
   2. With today's emphasis on cost containment in health care, staffing must be cost-effective, yet sufficient to meet client needs
   3. Staffing and work schedules greatly affect nurses' job satisfaction and productivity, which ultimately affects client care
   4. Insufficient or ineffective staffing or scheduling can cause discontent, frustration, stress, poor morale, increased turnover, and absenteeism

B. Applications to nursing
   1. The nurse manager must be able to provide adequate staffing, working within the constraints of cost containment
   2. The nurse manager also has an ethical and legal responsibility to provide sufficient staffing to ensure client safety
   3. Unsafe staffing practices, such as moving nurses to unfamiliar units or making nurses work double shifts, may create ethical or legal dilemmas for the nurse manager; for example, insufficient staffing may provide appropriate grounds for a client to sue for neglect
   4. A nurse manager should involve staff nurses in planning schedules whenever possible; this can help increase motivation and decrease absenteeism
   5. A nurse manager should never manipulate staffing schedules to punish employees; this is an unfair use of power
   6. If staff nurses are unionized, the nurse manager must consider any staffing patterns mandated by the labor contract
   7. In organizations that use centralized staffing systems, nurse leaders and managers should participate in staffing review committees to communicate staffing needs to higher management
   8. Decentralized staffing takes more time for a nurse manager; the nurse manager can save time by basing the staffing plan on an accepted staffing standard, such as the ANA's "Nursing Staff Requirements for In-Patient Health Care Services"

Points to remember

With today's emphasis on cost containment, quality care also must be cost-effective care.

Health care organizations, unlike other industries, must give 90 days' written notice before changes can be made in a labor contract.

A grievance may represent a violation of the labor contract or a misinterpretation of it, or it may be a means of expressing employee dissatisfaction.

Cost containment poses a significant challenge to nurses at all levels of a health care organization.

Inadequate staffing patterns may create legal and ethical dilemmas for a nurse manager.

Glossary

The following terms are defined in Appendix A, page 110.

arbitration

collective bargaining

grievance

Study questions

To evaluate your understanding of this chapter, answer the following questions in the space provided; then compare your responses with the correct answers in Appendix B, page 118.

1. What role does the National Labor Relations Board (NLRB) play in collective bargaining? _____

_____

2. How many days' notice must a health care organization receive before employees can strike? _____

_____

3. How would the practice of gainsharing affect cost containment at the unit level? _____

_____

4. How might inadequate staffing affect a nurse's job satisfaction and productivity? _____

_____

Appendices

A: Glossary

Accountability — assuming personal responsibility for actions and policies and accepting the consequences of one's behavior

Arbitration — process for settling labor disputes by involving a neutral third party, typically a labor relations expert

Associate nurse — nurse assigned to care for a primary nurse's client when the primary nurse is unavailable, following the primary nurse's care plan

Autocratic leadership — leadership style in which control rests entirely with the leader

Budget — funds allocated to an organization for ongoing and future use; an itemized summary of probable expenses and income for a given period; a tool for planning, monitoring, and controlling costs and meeting expenses; a plan for the use and evaluation of resources

Budget forecast — prediction of the activities of an organization over a set period of time, including such key items and expenses, revenues, materials, equipment, and personnel

Bureaucracy — complex organizational structure that relies on centralized power and authority; specialization of tasks; rigid rules, regulations, and hierarchy of authority; routine; formal communications; and detailed record keeping

Burnout — condition characterized by a lack of concern for one's work or profession that results from chronic, unrelieved, work-related stress

Capitation rate — hospital reimbursement system in which the hospital receives a flat rate for each member enrolled either through a health maintenance organization or a preferred provider organization

Case rate — hospital reimbursement system in which the hospital is paid a flat rate for each diagnosis

Centralized structure — organizational structure in which decisions are made at the top and handed down through management levels

Client acuity — psychological, biological, and medical status of a client; a basis for determining the intesity of care required

Client census – number of clients in a unit at any given time

Collective bargaining – process of negotiation between employees (usually through a union or employee association) and organizational management in an attempt to agree on employment terms and conditions

Cyclical work schedule – method of scheduling staff members using the same schedule repeatedly

Decentralized structure – employee-centered organizational structure in which decisions are made at the unit level

Decision package – device used in zero-based budgeting that lists all the activities of a given area, alternative ways of carrying out these activities and the cost for each, and the advantages of continuing and the consequences of discontinuing the activity; the activities are ranked from those essential to maintaining minimal operations to those nonessential but desirable

Decision rules – criteria used in the Vroom and Yetton model of decision making to identify an appropriate management style in a specific situation

Decision tree – diagram of the problem-solving process that identifies the primary problem and at least two alternative solutions

Democratic leadership – leadership style in which control is shared equally by the leader and group members

Diagnosis-related group (DRG) – system that classifies clients by age, medical diagnosis, and surgical procedure, to predict the use of hospital resources and length of stay and to sct predetermined Medicare reimbursement rates; DRGs are no longer used in New Jersey

Driving forces – forces that move the target of change in the desired direction

Empirical-rational strategy – strategy for handling minimal resistance to change; can be used to persuade the target to accept a rational change based on information about the change that is in the target's self-interest

Expenditures – monies listed on a budget as spent; also known as expenses

Feedback – in systems theory, the analysis and interpretation of output with the purpose of either reactivating or changing the system

Gainsharing – method of allowing employees to share in the economic success of a for-profit health care institution; stock ownership and profit sharing are similar options

"Great man" theory — leadership theory holding that great leaders are born and that the qualities of effective leadership are inherited and cannot be taught or learned

Grievance — substantial employee complaint to management, usually involving working conditions or contract violations

Group cohesiveness — degree of involvement that members of a group have with the group

Health maintenance organization (HMO) — prepaid system that provides a range of health care services in return for a preset initial joining fee

Health promotion — activities that enhance health and well-being

I-messages — technique for assertive communication that involves framing statements in personal terms, for example, "I'm becoming exasperated by your constant lateness."

Incident report — documentation of an event, usually an accident or injury, either client- or employee-related, that represents a risk for the organization

Incremental budgeting — method of budgeting that uses the expenditures from the previous year as a basis for the current annual budget

Input — in systems theory, the material and ideas received from the environment

Interactional theory — leadership theory that explores goal-oriented leadership and is concerned with predicting leader effectiveness

Laissez-faire leadership — leadership style in which control rests entirely with the group

Legitimate power — variable in the contingency model that refers to the leader's place within the organization and the amount of authority given to the leader by his or her official position as leader; also known as positional power

Line position — salaried position depicted in the organizational chart by solid vertical or horizontal lines

Marketing plan — written statement of a strategy that targets a specific audience and includes time-related details for carrying it out

Motivation — behavior that is goal directed; the establishment of goal-directed behaviors that satisfy individual needs

Moving—second step in the three-step process of planned change in which the target adopts a new pattern of behavior and the driving and restraining forces develop equilibrium

Normative-reeducative strategy—strategy for handling resistance to change that relies on interpersonal relations between the target and the change agent, with the aim of reeducating the target and altering norms and attitudes

Organization—group of people working together, under formal and informal rules of behavior, to achieve a common purpose; also the procedures, policies, and methods involved in achieving this common purpose

Output—in systems theory, the end product derived from receiving and processing of input

Per diem rate—hospital reimbursement system in which an HMO pays the hospital on a per-patient, per-day rate

Power—ability or capacity to substantially influence others' behavior

Power-coercive strategy—strategy for handling resistance to change that relies on authority and economic or political sanctions to enforce a change

Primary nurse—registered nurse responsible for the total care of a group of clients 24 hours a day from admission through discharge

Productivity—measure of both the quality and quantity of work done

Professional practice—governance structure in which a nursing unit becomes a self-sufficient, autonomously functioning business whose goals reflect efficient financial performance and quality assurance; these units may or may not have a nurse manager

Prospective payment system (PPS)—method of reimbursement from third-party payors to health care organizations, particularly hospitals, that is based on a client's diagnosis, with payment for services determined by DRGs

Refreezing—final step in the process of planned change, which occurs when the target has internalized and accepted the new pattern of behavior

Restraining forces—forces that impede change by moving the target of change in an undesired direction

Scheduler—person within the management structure with the authority and responsibility to assign staff; seen with centralized staffing

Self-governance—control of nursing services and their costs by nurses

Shared governance – means of involving staff nurses in all nursing-related decisions through participation in a formal nursing staff organization that establishes standards of practice, quality, education, management, research, and professionalism; the organizational structure consists of a nurse executive board and various councils and their committees

Situational theory – leadership theory proposing that essential traits for a leader vary depending on particular situations

Span of control – the number of employees a manager can effectively oversee

Staffing – function and process of determining and securing the nursing personnel required to provide safe, quality client care over a 24-hour period

Staff position – advisory or service position with little or no decision-making authority, depicted in the organizational chart by dotted horizontal lines

Standard – level of optimal performance that defines the scope and degree of nursing care necessary to ensure the quality of nursing care

Team leader – nurse assigned to care for a group of clients with the help of other nurses (team nurses) and ancillary personnel; he or she is responsible for supervising and coordinating all care provided by the team members

Throughput – in systems theory, the processing or transformation of input

Total Quality Management (TQM) – system of management that focuses on those processes that ensure organizational efficiency, effectiveness, and quality through organizational teamwork and excellence

Trait theory – leadership theory positing that qualities of effective leadership can be identified, taught, and learned

Transformational theory – leadership theory proposing that leaders and followers interact to achieve higher levels of motivation

Unfreezing – first step in the three-step process of planned change that results from the imbalance in the driving and restraining forces; the status quo is disrupted and new patterns of behavior must be developed

Variable work schedule – method of scheduling staff members by providing each nurse unit with a minimum number of staff members and increasing or decreasing that number according to the work load

B: Answers to Study Questions

CHAPTER 1

1. An organization's structure is determined by its operative organizational theory.

2. Classical organizational theory holds that the role of management is to increase production through close supervision of the work of others.

3. A parental leader fosters obedience and dependency in group members.

4. Planning is the most critical management function.

CHAPTER 2

1. Key elements of a bureaucracy include a centralized authority structure, highly specialized division of labor, rigid hierarchy of management, rigid rules and regulations, routine, formal communications, and detailed record keeping.

2. The Hawthorne experiment refers to research that discovered that various psychological and social factors in the work situation exerted more influence on productivity than did actual physical conditions.

3. The hallmark of modern organizational theory is the systems framework.

4. Modern organizational theory focuses on organizational processes rather than on structure.

CHAPTER 3

1. The philosophy of an organization forms the basis of the formal organizational structure.

2. Organizational structure can be centralized or decentralized.

3. Organizational climate refers to the employees' perception of the workplace.

4. Official, voluntary, and proprietary health care organizations are types of organizations categorized by their major source of funding.

CHAPTER 4

1. Case nursing is considered the oldest approach to client care.

2. Functional nursing reflects a bureaucratic, centralized organization.

3. A team leader is responsible for managing the care of a group of clients. He or she assigns personnel, plans and evaluates the nursing care provided by the team, and reports to the nurse manager.

4. Primary nursing reflects a decentralized organizational structure.

5. A critical path refers to a time frame used in managed care and takes into account the usual length of stay, interventions and their timing, resources needed, and expected client outcomes.

CHAPTER 5

1. According to the "great man" theory, leadership is inherited and cannot be taught or learned; that is, people are born to lead.

2. According to the trait theory, leadership qualities can be identified and taught to others. Specific personality traits are essential to leadership, including intelligence, knowledge, skill, energy and enthusiasm, initiative, self-confidence, patience, persistence, and empathy.

3. Group performance depends on the leader choosing an appropriate leadership style based on the four basic elements (organization, climate, leader characteristics, and follower characteristics) of the situation.

4. The tridimensional leadership effectiveness model focuses on leader behavior, group maturity, and leader effectiveness.

5. Transformational leadership attempts to create a meaningful, inspirational, and motivational workplace.

CHAPTER 6

1. The key ingredient in change is power.

2. When conflict occurs, it proceeds through five phases: perceived conflict, felt conflict, manifest conflict, conflict resolution or suppression, and conflict aftermath.

3. Group norms refer to a set of overt and covert standards that shape the behavior, attitudes, and perceptions of members.

4. Typically, downward communication involves messages that are primarily directive.

5. Self-competence is the ultimate form of power.

6. Two basic decision-making strategies are optimizing and satisfying.

CHAPTER 7

1. Team management, described as a great concern for both production and people, is considered ideal because it emphasizes the involvement of employees in all aspects of the managerial process.

2. The focus of management is enhanced productivity, which is achieved through uniform standards, effective feedback, and rewards for performance. Involving employees in those processes that affect them can increase employee commitment to enhanced productivity.

3. Fiedler's contingency model of managerial effectiveness is the only model to explore the concept of power as a key variable.

4. Participative management is possible only in a decentralized organizational structure.

5. Organizational teamwork and individual empowerment are essential to a Total Quality Management approach. However, neither are possible without managerial and administrative commitment to individual employee autonomy in decision making.

CHAPTER 8

1. Values clarification and assertiveness help increase self-awareness, self-confidence, and maturity, which are essential in establishing clear priorities and in delegating, through effective communication, the authority to carry out a delegated task. Priority setting and delegation are key to effective time management.

2. Benchmarking is the practice of measuring the overall effectiveness of a process by comparing it to similar processes. In performance appraisal, benchmarking involves selection of the best example of performance as a criterion to measure related performances. In Continuous Quality Improvement, benchmarking involves selection of a standard of excellence in a process or a procedure and using that standard to measure related processes or procedures.

3. The two standards emphasized by both Quality Assurance and Continuous Quality Improvement programs are outcome and process standards.

4. A mentor provides an individual with direction, counseling, and ongoing support in career development. Having a mentor paves the way for developing self-confidence and commitment to personal and professional self-actualization, which is the highest form of motivation.

CHAPTER 9

1. The desired outcome of any organizational budget is the optimal use of resources.

2. In zero-based budgeting, expenditures for the previous year are irrelevant; each year the budget starts at zero. Incremental budgeting uses previous year expenditures as the basis for the current budget.

3. In any organization, the two principal expenditures in an operating budget are personnel and supplies and equipment.

CHAPTER 10

1. Staffing is determined by the number and mix of personnel available, client census, type of client care delivery system in use, and levels of client acuity.

2. Patient classification systems, if properly managed, enable nurse managers to objectively quantify nursing care in terms of the "costing out" of nursing services. Costing out nursing services is essential for justifying the need for skilled nursing care and obtaining reimbursement for that care.

3. Decentralized staffing relates to Continuous Quality Improvement in that accountability is developed from the point of service upward through the administrative levels. Accountability for staffing, for example, takes place at the nursing unit level.

CHAPTER 11

1. Economic changes have resulted in federally mandated efforts to reduce expenditures; increased consumer demand for quality service; increased competition among health care organizations; and demand for cost containment, cost-effectiveness and health care provider excellence and accountability.

2. Demographic changes are necessitating a shift in nursing practice from hospital-based to community-based care, creating more independent and diversified nursing roles that require strong leadership and management skills.

3. The American Health Security Act of 1993 is a health care reform proposal introduced into Congress in an attempt to control rising health care costs and provide adequate health care coverage for all citizens.

CHAPTER 12

1. The National Labor Relations Board resolves disputes between an employer and a bargaining unit.

2. Health care organizations, because of their responsibility for client safety, must be given 10 days' notice before a strike can take place.

3. Providing employees with a financial incentive by allowing them to share in the profits of an institution is one way of making employees more conscious of efficiency measures and measures to reduce waste.

4. Inadequate staffing can cause discontent, frustration, stress, poor morale, increased turnover, and absenteeism.

Selected References

Barker, A.M. *Transformational Nursing Leadership*. Baltimore: Williams & Wilkins, 1990.

Bernhard, L., and Walsh, M. *Leadership, the Key to the Professionalization of Nursing*, 2nd ed. St. Louis: Mosby, Inc., 1990.

Grohar-Murray, M.E., and DiCroce, H.R. *Leadership and Management in Nursing*. Norwalk, Conn.: Appleton & Lange, 1992.

Hein, E.C., and Nicholson, M.J. *Contemporary Leadership Behavior: Selected Readings*, 4th ed. Philadelphia: J.B. Lippincott Co., 1994.

Joint Commission on Accreditation of Health Care Organizations. *Accreditation Manual for Hospitals* Oak Terrace, Ill.: JCAHO, 1992.

Kramer, M., and Schmalenburg, C. "Learning From Success: Autonomy and Empowerment," *Nursing Management* 24: 58-64, 1993.

Marquis, B.L., and Huston, C.J. *Leadership Roles and Management Functions in Nursing*. Philadelphia: J.B. Lippincott Co., 1992.

Marquis, B.L., and Huston, C.J. *Management Decision-Making for Nurses: 118 Case Studies*, 2nd ed. Philadelphia: J.B. Lippincott Co., 1994.

Sullivan, M., and Decker, P.S. *Effective Management in Nursing*, 3rd ed. Redwood City, Calif: Addison-Wesley Nursing, 1992.

Swansburg, R.C. *Management and Leadership for Nurse Managers*. Boston: Jones & Bartlett, 1990.

Tappen, R. *Nursing Leadership and Management*, 2nd ed. Philadelphia: F.A. Davis, 1989.

Zander, K. "Nursing Care Management: Strategic Management of Cost and Quality Outcomes," *Journal of Nursing Administration* 18: 23-30, 1993.

Index

t refers to a table.

t refers to a table.

---

t refers to a table.